SOCIAL STUDIES LEVEL 3

Exploring People and Society

Laura Anderson

Series Editor: Ollie Bray

DYNAMIC LEARNING

HODDER GIBSON
AN HACHETTE UK COMPANY

The Publishers would like to thank the following for permission to reproduce copyright material:
Photo credits:

p.3 Mark Henley/Photolibrary; p.4 © Neil Farrin/JAI/Corbis; p.5 © Noel Yates/Alamy; p.6 © Richard G. Bingham II/ Alamy; p.12 (l) © Hodder Gibson, (tl) © david pearson/Alamy, (bl) © Hodder Gibson; p.13 (l) © Icon Digital Featurepix/ Alamy, (r) © Lance Bellers/iStockphoto; p.14-15 © Laura Anderson; p.17 (t) © Kathy deWitt/Alamy, (c) © Kevin Britland/ Alamy, (b) © T.M.O.Buildings/Alamy; p.18 © Imagestate Media; p.19 © gaffera/iStockphoto; p.20 (l) © 1997 Tony Gable and C Squared Studios/Photodisc/Getty Images, (r) Getty Images; p.21 Susan Kinast/Getty Images; p.22 (t) © Janine Wiedel Photolibrary/Alamy, (b) © Clynt Garnham Lifestyle/Alamy; p.24 Getty Images NA; p.25 (t) © Jazz Archiv/Vas/ dpa/Corbis, (b) Getty Images; p.26 © Brand X/2010 Jupiterimages Corporation; p.27 (l) AFP/Getty Images, (r) AFP/Getty Images; p.30 © Brand X/2010 Jupiterimages Corporation; p.31 © Mary Evans Picture Library; p.32 © STEVE LINDRIDGE/ Alamy; p.33 (l) © Paul Fawcett/iStockphoto, (r) © Errol Hogenkamp/Fotolia; p.36 (SNP) (both) © Scottish National Party, (Labour) (l) © Steve Phillips/Alamy, (r) © Allstar Picture Library/Alamy, (b) © The Labour Party; p.37 (Conservative) (all) © The Conservative Party, (Liberal Democrats) (all) © The Liberal Democrat Party; p.41 © Adam Elder/Scottish Parliament; p.42 © Omar Sobhani/Reuters/Corbis; p.43 © STEPHEN HIRD/Reuters/Corbis; p.44 © Daily Record; p.46 AFP/Getty Images; p.47 (l) © Lance Bellers/iStockphoto,(r) Travelshots.com/Alamy; p.48 © JAMES FRASER/Rex Features; p.49 © PA Wire/Press Association Images; p.51 (l) © Epicscotland/Alamy, (r) DENNIS GILBERT/Photolibrary; p.56 © Gary Lucken/Alamy; p.58 © Human Rights Watch; p.59 © Amnesty International; p.61 © DVLA/Crown Copyright; p.62 © Colin Craig/Alamy; p.64 (l) © Stockbyte/Getty Images, (r) © John McKenna/Alamy; p.66 (l) © Mark Richardson/ iStockphoto, (r) © Monkey Business/Fotolia; p.68 (t) © Maritime and Coastguard Agency, (b) © Royal National Lifeboat Institution; p.70 (l) © Robert Harding Picture Library Ltd/Alamy, (r) © Swim Ink/Corbis; p.72 © Bob Sacha/Corbis; p.73 (l) © Jon Arnold Images Ltd/Alamy, (r) © Lou Linwei/Alamy; p.74 (l) China Photos/Getty Images, (r) AFP/Getty Images; p.75 © Peter Turnley/CORBIS; p.77 (l) © SCPhotos/Alamy, (r) © Michael S. Yamashita/CORBIS; p.78 © David Levenson/Alamy; p.79 © SALVATORE DI NOLFI/AP/Press Association Images; p.80 © jeremy sutton-hibbert/Alamy; p.81 ©Ellen B. Senisi/ The Image Works/Topfoto; p.82 CPC, Communist Party of China/Courtesy of Wikipedia Commons; p. 83 (t) © vario images GmbH & Co.KG/Alamy, (b) © Andia/Alamy; p.84 (l) © Eye Ubiquitous/Alamy; (r) © Bob Sacha/Corbis; p.85 © Diego Azubel/epa/Corbis; p.86 © NASA; p.89 AFP/Getty Images; p.90 © Mike Cassese/Reuters/Corbis; p.92 Image Source/ Getty Images; p.93 © Mike Russell/Alamy; p.94 (l) © Red Cross, (r) © Oxfam International; p.95 © Gideon Mendel/ ActionAid/Corbis; p.97 David Trood/Getty Images; p.99 Getty Images; p.100 © Design Pics Inc./Alamy; p.103 © Design Pics Inc./Alamy; p.104 CHRIS HELLIER/SCIENCE PHOTO LIBRARY; p.105 (l) AY LACEY/SCIENCE PHOTO LIBRARY, (r) Robert Lawson/Photlibrary, (b) PETER MENZEL/SCIENCE PHOTO LIBRARY; p.106 Gtorelly@Flickr.com; p.110 © David J. Green/Alamy; p.111 © Rob Collard; p.112-113 © Photodisc/Getty Images; p.114-115 (all) © Chicza; p.116 Joeszilagyi@ Flickr; p.117 © David Gee/Alamy; p.119 Courtesy of Straight plc.

Every effort has been made to trace all copyright holders, but if any have been inadvertently overlooked the Publishers will be pleased to make the necessary arrangements at the first opportunity.

Although every effort has been made to ensure that website addresses are correct at time of going to press, Hodder Gibson cannot be held responsible for the content of any website mentioned in this book. It is sometimes possible to find a relocated web page by typing in the address of the home page for a website in the URL window of your browser.

Hachette UK's policy is to use papers that are natural, renewable and recyclable products and made from wood grown in sustainable forests. The logging and manufacturing processes are expected to conform to the environmental regulations of the country of origin.

Orders: please contact Bookpoint Ltd, 130 Milton Park, Abingdon, Oxon OX14 4SB. Telephone: (44) 01235 827720. Fax: (44) 01235 400454. Lines are open 9.00–5.00, Monday to Saturday, with a 24-hour message answering service. Visit our website at www.hoddereducation.co.uk. Hodder Gibson can be contacted direct on: Tel: 0141 848 1609; Fax: 0141 889 6315; email: hoddergibson@hodder.co.uk

© Laura Anderson 2010
First published in 2010 by
Hodder Gibson, an imprint of Hodder Education,
An Hachette UK Company
2a Christie Street
Paisley PA1 1NB

Impression number   5 4 3
Year   2014 2013 2012

Cover photo © Janine Wiedel / Photofusion
Illustrations by Emma Golley at Redmoor Design, Metaphrog and Jeff Edwards
Typeset in Stone Serif (11pt) by DC Graphic Design Limited
Printed in Italy

A catalogue record for this title is available from the British Library

ISBN: 978 1444 112771

Contents

1 Why is it important to study Modern Studies?

Modern Studies is just politics, foreign countries and war!

Modern Studies is about all of those things, but it is also about a lot more. It is a way of looking at the world. Its focus is people and the way they interact. You will learn to look at the world locally, nationally and internationally. Locally refers to the area around your home. This could be your town, village or local council area. Nationally refers to the whole of Scotland or Britain. Internationally refers to the whole world.

Modern Studies is all about understanding society by examining how it changes, how it is run and what can influence it. Modern Studies will encourage you to become open-minded, tolerant and understanding of others and will help you become an active citizen.

Activate your brain cells!

Let's think about that for a minute ...

- Why is studying other people important?
- How do we find out about things that are going on?
- Are the people that report the news powerful?
- How do the people who run this country get the job?
- How powerful are the people who run this country?
- Think about all of these things. Now think really hard ... How can studying others change the way you think?

How can studying people help me with my future?

Modern Studies joins up with Geography and History to help you discover how your community, country and world have developed into what they are today.

Modern Studies is challenging because you always have to think about the other side of the argument.

Modern Studies helps you to understand other people's lives in far away countries and close to home.

You don't know how lucky you are until you learn about other people's experiences of life.

Modern Studies forces you to think in a different way.

The social subjects provide you with the skills to get a job.

Modern Studies helps you to understand the world.

Modern Studies is exciting because you can ask your teacher about anything that you see on the TV or in a newspaper.

Modern Studies is brilliant because there is usually no right answer and you get to debate things.

Show your understanding

1. Think about the students' statements about Modern Studies. Which one do you like the idea of the most?
2. Write a list of the statements and rank them, with the one you like most at the top and the one you are least interested in at the bottom.
3. Share your ideas with the rest of the class and your teacher. Can you reach an agreement as a class on one statement that best explains the importance of Modern Studies?

Skills for life!

Here we will focus on the skills you will learn in Modern Studies – the things you will get better at as we go through the book. Keep your skills work somewhere safe – the back of your jotter is a good idea. These skills are not simply subject skills but skills you will need throughout school and in life. Who says Modern Studies is not important?

Collect a skill

Increase your word power!

This skill is all about words. You will come across many words in this book which you may not have read or heard before. Learning how to spell them and what they mean will **increase your word power** and really help you to communicate with other people.

When you find a word in **bold** or in a glossary box or an idea you don't understand, record it in a vocabulary list. Explain its meaning in words and/or pictures. Ask your teacher or use a dictionary or encyclopaedia to help you understand the meaning.

Remind yourself to do this for all the chapters in the book to **boost your skill level!**

REVIEW Some schools in Scotland do not teach Modern Studies and no schools in England teach the subject. Think about why learning about society is so important and then imagine you have to explain it to someone who does not know what Modern Studies is. Try to explain it in three sentences.

2 What do I need to know to study Modern Studies?

What are we exploring?

By the end of this chapter you should be able to:

▶ Tell the difference between the terms 'social', 'economic' and 'political'

▶ Find out about your local area

Social, economic or political?

In Modern Studies we divide topics into things that are social, economic and political.

Social is all about people. For example, the differences in people's lifestyles.

Political is all about government. For example, the way in which Parliament works.

Economic is all about money. For example, why some people are poor and others are rich.

What is society?

Modern Studies examines how people live in society. The word society means a group of people who share certain features or characteristics. This could be all those people in a particular country who share a common past or culture. For example, people from Scotland generally believe they are part of a Scottish society – they share the same language, past and culture.

Within each society there are many different communities. People in a community are connected in some way. For example, members of the Chinese community in Scotland are connected by their common culture, language and past. So are the Irish, Muslim, Indian and Pakistani communities. Most people belong to more than one community at a time. Your school, village or town, religion and race are all types of communities.

St. Johns Village Community Notice Board

How do I find out about my local area?

Studying your local area is an important skill to learn for any subject. There are many different ways to find out about your local community. One way to discover more is to read local newspapers. Local and regional newspapers will often report stories that are important on a small scale but that might not be big enough to be reported on a national scale. Most local newspapers nowadays have their own websites where you can find out more. Try going online and typing your hometown or regional newspaper into a search engine. You could also find out which papers are published in your area by asking a local newsagent.

Another way to find out about your local area is to use your local council or community council website. Local council websites will usually have facts and figures about your area, such as population figures for towns and villages and how many people are unemployed or how many people are of school age. Your community council website will have minutes from all of their meetings. Minutes are records of meetings and will tell you about important things that are being discussed and events that are happening in your local area.

Your local library and librarian are also good sources of information. Notice boards will have posters about clubs and activities available locally. Your library will have lots of books and leaflets about your local area.

Finally, an important source of information is local people. Asking your parents, teachers or neighbours about the area is often the best way to find out information that may not be written down in sources. If your grandparents live locally they may be able to tell you a lot about how the area used to be. Knowing about the past is important to understand the present.

Stretch yourself

There are many different ways to find out about your local area. Make up a leaflet for a person who has just moved into your local area containing important information you think they might need to know.

 Show your understanding

1. Copy and complete the table below using the word bank to help.

Social (people)	Political (parliament)	Economic (money)

Who cares for the elderly? Who is the Prime Minister? How much do unemployed people get from the government? How much is the basic state pension? How are laws made? Why are some countries poor? What is racism? Why are some people poor? What is an election? Are people's lifestyles different?

2. What is the difference between society and community?
3. List the different ways you can find out about your local area.
4. For each method think of an advantage and a disadvantage.
5. Write down four questions you might ask people to find out how your local area has changed in the last 10, 20 or 50 years.

How do I carry out a survey?

What are we exploring?

By the end of this section you should be able to:

▶ Write questions suitable for a survey
▶ Record survey results
▶ Present and **analyse** results

A key part of Modern Studies is finding out about other people and what they think. One way of collecting information about other people is to carry out a survey or questionnaire.

> **Analyse** to study or examine something in detail in order to discover more about it.

Surveys and questionnaires are very useful because they provide up-to-date information that is often difficult to find from other sources. Surveys and questionnaires can also be designed to ask specific questions that are personal to your study. A survey is usually short, just a few questions, and is asked verbally. A questionnaire contains more questions and would be filled out on paper or online by the person responding.

One disadvantage of questionnaires is that they can take a lot of time to prepare, carry out and analyse. In order to get an accurate result a lot of people are required.

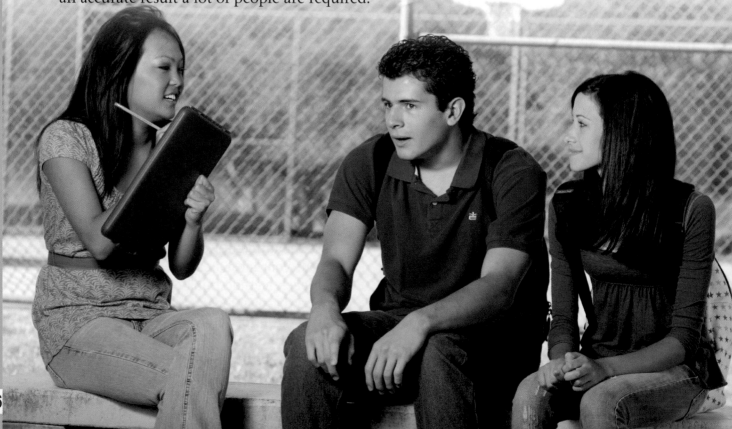

 **Collect a skill**

How do I carry out a class survey?

Step 1: Choosing a topic

It is important to choose a topic that will interest people so that they listen carefully and give accurate answers. Always choose a topic that you are interested in yourself so that you do not get bored before you are finished.

Below is a list of topics to get you started.

Hobbies   Pets
Films   Sports
Music   Holidays

Now choose your topic.

Step 2: Designing a question

Often surveys will have more than one question but for this class survey you only need one question. Writing a survey question is more difficult than you might think. Remember you are going to need to record answers quickly so that you have time to ask everyone in the class. You might wish to make your question multiple-choice so that you can just make a tally mark next to the correct answer.

Now write your question.

Step 3: Asking your question and recording the results

When your teacher says that everyone is ready, you will get the chance to ask your question. Here are some important things to remember:

- Speak clearly so that your classmates know exactly what you are asking.
- Do not make one answer sound better than another. Every good survey should remain impartial.
- Do not put words into people's mouths. Even your best friend might surprise you with a different answer.

- Carefully record your results so that you do not get confused when it is time to analyse them.

Step 4: Analysing your results

Now it is time to look at your results in detail. Answer the following questions:

- What was the most popular answer?
- What was the least popular answer?
- Can you think of any reasons why?
- Are you surprised by the answers? Give reasons why.

Step 5: Presenting your results

Survey results can be presented in lots of different ways. One of the simplest is to use a bar graph for each question. Draw a bar graph of your results. It should look something like this.

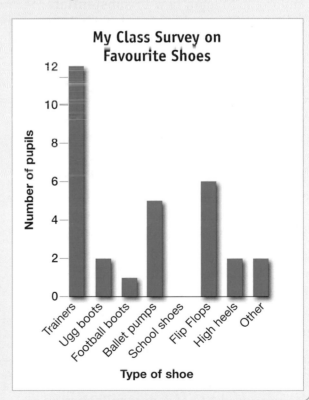

REVIEW Make a list of four important things to remember when carrying out a survey.

4 How do I write a report?

What are we exploring?

By the end of this section you should be able to:

▶ Read text and extract relevant information

▶ Evaluate points of view and make a decision

▶ Provide evidence to support your decision

Decision making exercise: Proposed wind farm in the north-west Highlands

Substantiate back up with evidence.

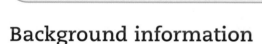 **Collect a skill**

Learning to make decisions is a key skill both in Modern Studies and in life. It is important to learn how to **substantiate** your decisions. This exercise will help to teach you this skill.

 Activate your brain cells!

Carefully read the background information on Portbyrne and all of the sources. Think about the importance of each source as you read.

Background information

Portbyrne is a small village of approximately 5000 people in the north-west Highlands of Scotland. The community traditionally farmed the local landscape and fished in the waters of Loch Ballach. Nowadays only a few people still farm or fish. Most people work in the service industry in local shops, cafes and hotels. Many people can only find work in the summer months when tourists are visiting the area. Unemployment is high and poverty is increasing. Many families are moving away from the area because they cannot get jobs locally.

The proposed site at Achnaballach used to be a part of the neighbouring Nostbuie Estate, which is famous for its grouse shooting. When Mr MacDonald died in 1999 the land was left to the Portbyrne Community Council. The land is mainly heather moorland above 300m.

Source 1: Location of proposed windfarm

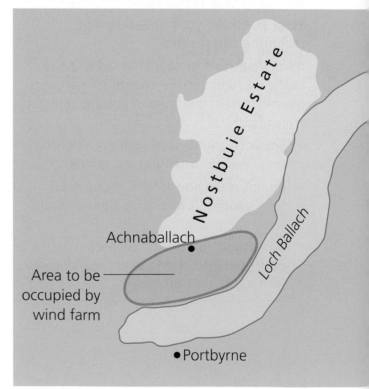

Source 2: Newspaper article from *The Portbyrne Record*

Cleanair to rescue local economy

International energy giant Cleanair yesterday announced plans to build a new wind farm north of the village of Portbyrne. The land at Achnaballach is of little economic value to the local people and has sat idle since 1999.

The construction of the wind farm will take six months to a year, bringing much-needed employment opportunities to the area. Cleanair have promised to hire local people during construction and afterwards to maintain the turbines and manage the site. Unemployment has risen steadily in Portbyrne over recent years and this is just the investment the village needs.

Cleanair is a Dutch company with many years of experience building wind farms in rural areas. Jan Rotmensen, a spokesperson for the company, said yesterday, 'The utmost care will be taken to preserve the natural landscape and environment around the site. It will bring jobs to Porthyrne as well as clean energy for the future.'

The new wind farm will produce enough green energy to power 210,000 homes in Scotland. This means the entire village of Portbyrne could be run on Cleanair's energy, making it one of the greenest villages in Scotland. The excess energy will be sold to the National Grid so that it will be contributing to the Scottish Government's emissions targets for 2050.

Portbyrne will be able to re-market itself as a green holiday destination, where people can enjoy a holiday safe in the knowledge that they are not contributing to the destruction of the planet. The green holiday market is expanding at a rapid pace and Cleanair have just given local people the chance to offer something new to holidaymakers.

There will be a public meeting on Wednesday 14th May to discuss Cleanair's plans for the site at Achnaballach. Jan Rotmensen will be there to represent the company and answer all enquiries from local people.

Source 3: Newspaper article from *The West Coast Gazette*

Achnaballach ecosystem under threat!

Yesterday saw the announcement of a new wind farm to be erected on the site of Achnaballach. Dutch-based energy company Cleanair has bid to take over the site north of the village. Cleanair has a reputation for building giant wind farms in rural settings throughout Europe; each site aiming to be record-breaking in size.

The plans for the land involve an ugly site office and 160 wind turbines standing at a height of 80 metres. The wind farm will dwarf the surrounding landscape and will completely cover the land at Achnaballach.

There is little in Cleanair's history that suggests that they are concerned about the local community or local landscape. Cleanair is a company which is out to break records and make profits. Jan Rotmensen, spokesperson for the company, looked uncomfortable making the statement to the press. He came across as nervous and inexperienced.

Morag MacAndrew of the local B&B association had this to say this afternoon: 'We are extremely concerned by Cleanair's plans. The wind farm will damage the local landscape and will be a massive scar on the beautiful views which draw tourists to the village.'

Mrs MacAndrew is not the only one concerned by today's announcement. The West Highland Wildlife Club (WHWC) has also expressed its concerns. 'The ecosystem at Achnaballach is a delicate one. Rare species such as the capercaillie live in the moorland on the estate. What may look like a worthless piece of land is vital to the survival of such species. We don't yet know the full effects of wind farms on bird populations and certainly have no data for a site of this size,' said James McIntyre, President of the WHWC.

It looks like the public meeting on Wednesday might be more difficult for Cleanair than they anticipated when they sent a junior associate to represent the company.

Source 4: Statement from local constituency MSP Charles Hamilton

I am the local MSP for Portbyrne and surrounding area. I can see both points of view in this case and am unsure what to recommend to the Portbyrne Community Council.

Portbyrne is a community of high unemployment with increasing numbers of families moving away from the area to search for work. This puts pressure on the local schools and the Highland Council are beginning to consider closing Portbyrne High School. Pupils would then have to be bussed 45 miles to the High School in Inverballarine.

However, there are issues surrounding the reputation of Cleanair that concern me. I would like to see further evidence that the wind farm will not damage local bird populations. I am also concerned that the wind farm will harm the tourist industry because of the disruption to the view from the village.

Finally, I am aware that as an MSP I must also think about Scotland as a whole. The Scottish Government have set tough emissions targets for 2050 and this wind farm would be a significant step towards achieving these targets. I look forward to the meeting on Wednesday night so that I can hear from my constituents.

Source 5: Letters to the Editor of *The West Highland Courier*

Dear Sir,

I am extremely concerned about Cleanair's plans to build an ugly wind farm which would be visible from my house. I am worried it would damage the value of my house and put people off coming to my B&B. I rely on the money I make in the summer months to last me through the winter.

Yours sincerely,
Shona Anderson

Dear Sir,

I think the wind farm sounds like a brilliant idea. I grew up in Portbyrne and am a teacher at the High School. We need families to remain in the local area so that the school does not close. The wind farm will bring lots of new jobs and will attract green tourists to the area.

Yours truly,
Hamish MacLeod

Dear Sir,

I am totally against the new wind farm. It will damage the environment around the site and threaten the rare capercaillie bird. Not enough research has been carried out on the effects of wind farms on bird populations.

Yours sincerely,
Douglas James

Dear Sir,

I am 25 and have lived in Portbyrne all of my life. I do not want to leave. I work in the hotel in the summer and work a few shifts for them in the winter but they cannot keep me on full time. Every year I try hard to find work and there are never enough jobs to go around. If something doesn't change soon I will have to move away. They have promised to hire local people. I need the wind farm to go ahead.

Yours,
Danny Bruce

Dear Sir,

I live on the Nostbuie Estate next to Achnaballach. I have a young family and am concerned that the construction of the wind farm will bring heavy machinery along the single track road outside my home. I am also really worried that the wind farm itself will be noisy after it is built.

Yours sincerely,
Sarah MacLean

Dear Sir,

I live in Portbyrne and have studied climate change to university level. People must stop thinking about the immediate impact of such wind farms and stop worrying about their views. If we do not start using alternative energy now then there will be far bigger problems as a result of climate change than a slightly different view. I think wind farms are beautiful in their own way and would attract people to the local area.

Sincerely,
Jane Hamilton

Collect a skill

Copy and complete the table below to help you identify all of the arguments surrounding the wind farm development. Make sure you keep a record of where the information came from. The first one has been done for you.

Arguments for	Arguments against
Portbyrne has high unemployment. Wind farm will bring jobs. (Source 2)	

Read Source 4 carefully. The MSP is undecided about the wind farm. How many different influences does the MSP have to consider? Make a list in your jotter.

Imagine you have been hired by the Chairperson of Portbyrne Community Council to help her decide whether to recommend the wind farm or not.

You must evaluate all of the sources and write a report summarising all of the arguments on both sides. In your conclusion you must either recommend or reject the proposed wind farm.

Make sure you explain clearly why you have made this decision.

Your report should have the following headings:

- **Introduction:** Who are you? What have you been asked to do? Include some background information on Portbyrne.
- **Arguments for the wind farm.**
- **Arguments against the wind farm.**
- **Conclusion:** Remember to include reasons to support your decision.

5 What is Scottish identity?

What are we exploring?

By the end of this chapter you should be able to:
▶ Explain how culture and identity are connected
▶ Give examples of Scottish customs

A person's identity is based on where they were born, what they eat, the music they listen to, the beliefs they hold and their history. Scottish identity is connected to all of these but also to the belief that Scotland is home. It relates to the fact that the people in Scotland have a common culture, a common language and a common history.

Activate your brain cells!

Draw a small picture of yourself. Around the picture write words to describe your identity.

What does it mean to have a common culture?

The word culture refers to the ideas, customs, food and arts of a particular group of people; in this case, Scots. Sharing a common culture means to practise the same traditions such as celebrating Burns' Night with haggis, neeps and tatties. The fact that Scottish men wear kilts to special occasions is something that brings Scots together. The playing of the bagpipes is another custom that people from around the world identify as being Scottish. Wearing tartan is also a Scottish custom, as is celebrating Hogmanay. Scottish culture also includes lots of typical foods and drinks such as whisky, Irn Bru and shortbread. Culture also includes art and literature and there are many famous Scots who have contributed to Scottish culture: Sir Walter Scott, Sir Arthur Conan Doyle, Robert Burns and even J. K. Rowling.

What does history have to do with identity?

A country's identity is closely linked to its history. Having a common past binds people together and gives them a sense of belonging. The traditions and symbols around which Scottish identity is based all come from the history of Scotland. Scotland is famous around the world for its many castles.

The flag of Scotland is a white-on-blue diagonal cross called the Saltire. It is based on the cross on which St Andrew (the patron saint of Scotland) was crucified. According to legend, in AD832 a battle was fought in East Lothian near the village of Athelstaneford. An army of Picts and Scots under the High King of Alba, Angus MacFergus, was invading East Lothian, which belonged to Northumbria at that time. On the morning of the battle, King Angus saw a white cloud in the shape of the cross on a blue sky background and thought that it was a sign. He stated that if he won the battle then St Andrew would be the patron saint of Scotland and the Saltire would be the national flag. Angus was the winner!

Another important Scottish symbol is the thistle. It is almost as Scottish as tartan or bagpipes. It has been an important Scottish symbol for more than 500 years and first appeared on silver coins in the reign of James III in 1470. Nobody really knows how the thistle became a Scottish symbol but one legend tells of a group of sleeping Scots warriors who were about to be attacked by a band of Vikings when one of the Vikings stood on a thistle. His cries raised the alarm and the Scots defeated the invaders. In gratitude, the plant became known as the 'Guardian Thistle' and was adopted as the symbol of Scotland.

What does it mean to share a common language?

The third aspect of identity is language. The English language is spoken throughout Scotland. This means that no matter where in Scotland you are, you can communicate easily with other Scots. There are other languages that bring people in Scotland together. In the Highlands and Islands, Gaelic is widely spoken. In the North-East many people speak a local dialect called Doric. And there are still an estimated 1.6 million people who speak Scots, the ancient language of Robert Burns.

It is not just the English language that is common to all Scots but also the slang words that have become a part of Scottish English. Some of these have Scots origins. 'Hogmanay', 'neeps' and 'tatties' are three words already mentioned but there are many more.

 Show your understanding

1. What are the three parts of identity?
2. Read the section on culture. Now list as many Scottish customs as you can. Try to come up with some that are not in the text.
3. Why does Scotland have the Saltire as its flag?
4. Why is history important to identity?
5. Now use your imagination. Think of a person who is the epitome (ultimate example) of Scottish identity. Either write a paragraph describing her/him or draw her/him and label your drawing with describing words.

? Bore your friends...

The Bank of Scotland was the first bank in Europe to print its own money.

Stretch yourself

There are lots of words that are Scottish English. Work with a partner and see how many you can list.

6 Do people in Scotland have different lifestyles?

What are we exploring?

By the end of this section you should be able to:

► Understand the difference between the terms urban and rural
► Identify the factors that influence lifestyle
► Describe your lifestyle

What is Scotland really like?

Although Scotland is a small country, it has a diverse landscape and people experience different lifestyles depending upon where they live and work.

While the majority of Scotland's population lives in the urban areas of the central belt of Scotland, many others live in rural Scotland far away from the cities. The central belt of Scotland runs from Glasgow in the west to Edinburgh in the east. The word urban describes the built-up areas of towns and cities. Rural describes the countryside and includes villages and hamlets.

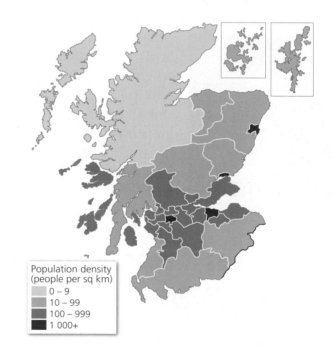

Population density (people per sq km)
- 0 – 9
- 10 – 99
- 100 – 999
- 1 000+

What is lifestyle?

Lifestyle is the way a person lives their life and includes job, hobbies, clothes, car, music, food, exercise, house and holidays. There are many factors that influence a person's lifestyle choices, including money, age, religious beliefs, family responsibilities, education, geographic location and health.

Some people have a lot of control over their lifestyle and can choose to spend their time and money in a way that suits them. Others are not so lucky and may not be able to live the lifestyle they want. For example, a young single mother may want a lifestyle of luxurious holidays, designer clothes and spa days but may not have the money or support to afford it. Similarly, a young Muslim boy may want to go out clubbing and drinking but his religion forbids it.

Plockton High School

Plockton, in the north-west highlands

Rural Scotland

Around 27 per cent of Scotland's population live in rural areas. People in these areas have different lifestyles and therefore different needs from those in urban areas. Take, for example, the area of Lochalsh in the north-west Highlands.

There is only one secondary school in Lochalsh: Plockton High School. People come from many miles around to go to school in Plockton. Some travel so far that they have to stay in a hostel during the week. The school has a total enrolment of approximately 300 pupils and around 40 staff.

The pupils of Plockton High School have limited choices in their lifestyles. The only shops nearby are craft shops, galleries and local food stores. Teenagers fill their time sailing or playing football in the summer, playing badminton or taking part in drama in the winter. Teenagers in Plockton have to travel 80 miles to Inverness to go shopping, or they do their shopping on the Internet.

Urban Scotland

Most of Scotland's population live in urban areas. Look at the example of Musselburgh Grammar School. Musselburgh is a 10-minute train ride away from the capital city of Edinburgh and all its attractions. The school roll is approximately 1400 with around 100 staff.

Musselburgh Grammar pupils spend their free time in lots of different ways. There are more activities available to them than there are in rural areas. There are lots of local clubs near to the school that offer pupils the chance to train in their favourite sport, such as football, dancing or rugby. Teenagers also have the option of going to the cinema, shopping or going for a pizza.

Musselburgh Grammar School

Musselburgh, East Lothian

Activate your brain cells!

What is lifestyle? Think about your own lifestyle. How would you explain the concept of lifestyle in your own words?

Show your understanding

1. Where do most people in Scotland live? Why do you think this is?
2. Explain the difference between urban and rural.
3. What is lifestyle?
4. Draw a spider diagram to show the main factors that influence lifestyle.
5. What are the main differences between life in Plockton and life in Musselburgh?
6. Describe your own lifestyle. Do you live in an urban area or rural area?

? Bore your friends ...

In Scotland, Irn Bru is more popular than Coke. When McDonald's opened in Glasgow and didn't serve Irn Bru it was considered an insult and some people boycotted the company.

Stretch yourself

Now imagine that you are 21 and money is no object. Describe your lifestyle.

What does a multicultural Scotland look like?

By the end of this section you should be able to:

▶ Understand what multicultural means

▶ Give evidence to support the idea that Scotland is multicultural

For a country to be multicultural it must be home to many different cultures and identities living side by side in peace. The idea behind multicultural living is that each of the cultures is celebrated alongside one another without losing its own identity. This means that all cultures are equal but still distinct.

An example of how multicultural Scotland has become is the fact that we now consider traditional food dishes from other cultures to be everyday foods in our diet – think of curry, pizza and chow mein.

 Activate your brain cells!

Discuss with a partner some of the things that may get in the way of a multicultural society.

How does a country become multicultural?

Scotland has always had a culture based on welcoming hospitality. For thousands of years, people have come to live in the country we now call Scotland. Even the word 'Scot' originally comes from people who migrated to Scotland from Northern Ireland around AD500.

Recently Scotland has been described as a multicultural country; it now has a variety of different cultures living side by side. There are many different immigrant communities in Scotland and with each generation they are becoming more integrated into Scottish society.

There is also a growth in the number of European immigrants coming to Scotland. This is especially true since 2004, when 10 new countries joined the European Union (EU).

Learning link

Am I European?

Many of the countries that joined the EU in 2004, such as Poland, Lithuania and Latvia, have a lower standard of living than Scotland so people come to Scotland to earn better wages, live in better housing and gain access to better health care and education.

So what does a multicultural Scotland look like?

Scotland's cities now have thriving communities of Polish, Italian and Indian immigrants. Walking around any of Scotland's cities you can see evidence of the growth of these communities in the delicatessens, restaurants and bookshops.

Statistics show that the number of people living in Scotland who were born abroad went up between 2004 and 2007. The five most common countries of birth for people living in Scotland in 2007, other than Scotland itself, were Poland, Germany, the Republic of Ireland, India and the United States of America.

Modern Scottish schools contain a mix of cultures from all over the world, often with many different languages being spoken and many different colours of skin. This further highlights Scotland's move towards becoming a multicultural country.

Recent estimates of Poles living in Scotland range from 40,000 to 100,000. The effects can be seen not just in the growth of new businesses but also by the fact that well-known supermarkets have begun to stock Polish foods.

Show your understanding

1. What does the term multicultural mean?
2. Why do people from other countries come to live in Scotland?
3. Which five countries have most new immigrants to Scotland come from?
4. Imagine you are leaving Scotland forever and going to live in another country. You can choose any country in the world. Write a diary entry about how you feel. What will you miss most about Scotland? What are you most looking forward to? What are you nervous about? How do you feel about going to school in a foreign country?

REVIEW

Do you think that Scotland is a multicultural society? Provide evidence to support your answer from your own village/town/city.

? Bore your friends ...

Scotland's longest place name is Coignafeuinternich!

Am I European?

By the end of this section you should be able to:

▶ Describe what the European Union is

▶ Discuss what a European identity is

▶ Make decisions about your identity

People from Scotland have several different identities: Scottish, British and European. People from Italy, Belgium, Poland and other mainland European countries have a strong European identity. However, Britain is an island and many British people feel detached from mainland Europe. So, are Scots European or not?

1 Albania	24 Italy
2 Andorra	25 Latvia
3 Armenia	26 Liechtenstein
4 Austria	27 Lithuania
5 Azerbaijan	28 Luxembourg
6 Belarus	29 Macedonia
7 Belgium	30 Moldova
8 Bosnia-Herzegovina	31 Monaco
9 Britain	32 Montenegro
10 Bulgaria	33 Netherlands
11 Croatia	34 Norway
12 Cyprus	35 Poland
13 Czech Republic	36 Portugal
14 Denmark	37 Romania
15 Estonia	38 Russia
16 Finland	39 Serbia
17 France	40 Slovakia
18 Georgia	41 Slovenia
19 Germany	42 Spain
20 Greece	43 Sweden
21 Hungary	44 Switzerland
22 Iceland	45 Turkey
23 Ireland	46 Ukraine

What is the European Union (EU)?

Activate your brain cells!

Do you feel European? Why? Why not?

The EU or European Union is a group of 27 countries that work together to improve the lives of the people that live in the EU area. The EU was originally started in 1957 to try to rebuild Europe following the destruction of the Second World War. Many cities had been damaged by bombing during the war and the infrastructure of the countries was damaged. Infrastructure includes the basic systems and services, such as transport and power supplies, that a country uses in order to work effectively.

The EU aims to promote peace and stability and to ensure that the people of Europe never have to live through another war. The founders of the EU thought that if countries traded (bought and sold goods from each other) and if people travelled between countries then they would become friendly and less likely to go to war.

The EU is based on the three freedoms of movement: people, goods and money. What this means is that all citizens of the EU can move around all 27 countries in the EU and live and work in any one they please. In Scotland this has meant that large numbers of people from other EU countries have come to make their homes in Scotland.

What is European identity?

If identity is based on a common culture, language and history then it is easy to see why Scottish people struggle to see themselves as European.

A common culture

Culture includes food, art, literature, music and other traditions. A common culture is becoming easier to recognise throughout Europe. Italian paintings hang in Scottish, French and Spanish galleries. Music from Spanish and Italian singers can be heard on Scottish radio stations. Food from Greece, France and Spain is served in Scottish homes and restaurants.

Another feature of culture which is bringing European countries together is the Euro. The Euro is a currency created by the Maastricht Treaty of the EU in 1992. It was

introduced to make the EU a stronger world power and to help the economies of the EU grow. A common currency is an important factor in European identity. The countries which have adopted the Euro as their currency are known as the Eurozone. Britain does not use the Euro as its currency.

Learning link

What are international problems?

A common language

There are 41 languages spoken throughout Europe. Within Britain alone there are three languages spoken: English, Welsh and Scottish Gaelic. In mainland Europe you can walk a few steps from one country to another and be faced with a completely different language. While French, Spanish and Italian share similar words and all have their origins in Latin, other languages are completely different and even have a different alphabet, such as Greek.

A common history

Although there are many events in history that all Europeans share – such as the rise and fall of the Roman and British Empires, and the two World Wars – the reality is that European countries have been split by historic events. For example, in the Second World War, Italy and Germany were on one side and Britain, France, Poland and Greece were on the other. This shows that prior to the 1950s, European countries did not share a common history and this had a negative impact on European identity.

 Collect a skill

Support and oppose!

One key skill in Modern Studies is to be able to **support and oppose** a point of view.

Discuss with a partner whether Scottish people can feel European. Make a list of arguments for and against the point of view.

 Show your understanding

1. What is the EU?
2. Why did the EU begin?
3. Upon which three freedoms is the EU based?
4. What is culture? Is there any evidence of a shared European culture?
5. How many languages are spoken in Europe?
6. Why is it difficult to describe European history as shared?

REVIEW Do you think there is a strong European identity? Provide reasons for your answer.

9 Why do people hate?

People hate for different reasons. Often people hate because they do not understand why people are different from them and as a result they are scared. Fear or hatred of people from other countries is called xenophobia.

Activate your brain cells!

Discuss with a partner the things that make people hate.

In modern Scotland there are many different cultures living and working together. Each culture has different traditions. Traditions are beliefs and customs that are handed down from one generation to the next. Often traditions are connected to religions. Before examining other cultures that now exist in Scotland, it is important to be able to identify Scottish traditions.

Learning link

What does a multicultural Scotland look like?

What are Scottish traditions?

Some traditions are on a small scale and may be traditions for only your own family, such as where you sit at the dinner table or opening your smallest Christmas present at midnight on Christmas Eve. Other traditions are large-scale and lots of people recognise them, such as eating haggis, neeps and tatties on Burns' Night, wearing a kilt to special occasions, or playing the bagpipes at celebrations, weddings and funerals.

What traditions from other cultures are now celebrated in Scotland?

As Scotland develops into a multicultural society, more and more traditions from other countries are becoming a part of life here. One such example would be the celebration of Chinese New Year. In 2010, Chinese New Year was celebrated on 14 February. Chinese New Year, also known as the Spring Festival, is one of the most important and oldest festivals for Chinese

people. The date on which it is celebrated changes because it is the start of the lunar year and so is determined by the stages of the Moon.

Traditionally, Chinese New Year is a time for families to come together. The festival focuses on food and good fortune. Families start their preparations as much as a month in advance, cleaning their homes to get rid of any bad luck. Hair is cut and new clothes and shoes are bought to symbolise a new start. Homes are then decorated with red paper scrolls with good luck greetings and blessings for the New Year.

The fifteen days of celebration are filled with feasting. The eve of the Spring Festival is the most important. The meal lasts until after midnight so that good luck can be carried over into the New Year. Each dish has a special meaning usually relating to wealth, health or prosperity.

On the last day of the celebrations, day fifteen, there is a lantern festival. This takes place under a full Moon. Multi-coloured paper lanterns in many shapes and sizes (dragons, butterflies and other animals) are displayed as the dragon and lion dance and parades pass through the streets.

Each New Year in China represents a new sign of the zodiac. This is unlike in Scotland, where the signs of the zodiac are assigned to months. The twelve Chinese signs of the zodiac are Rat, Ox, Tiger, Rabbit, Dragon, Snake, Horse, Goat, Monkey, Rooster, Dog and Pig. The year 2009 was the year of the Ox and 2010 was the year of the Tiger.

As well as Chinese New Year, other cultural traditions that are becoming more visible in Scotland include Muslims wearing headscarves and Sikhs wearing turbans.

Often hate can stem from a lack of understanding about different people's traditions and cultures. People hate what they don't know because they think it may threaten their own views, culture and traditions.

In order to successfully achieve a multicultural society in Scotland the government needs to address hatred. As hate comes from a fear of the unknown, educating people about other cultures is perhaps the simplest way to stop people hating.

Show your understanding

1. The text gives two examples of family traditions. Think about your own family and see how many family traditions you can list.
2. Traditions vary across the country. List as many local and Scottish (national) traditions as you can.
3. What is xenophobia?
4. Copy and complete the factfile about the Chinese New Year. Now make a factfile for a traditional Scottish New Year.

   > **Factfile: Chinese New Year**
   > Date celebrated:
   > Length of celebration:
   > Preparations:
   > Foods:
   > Traditions:

5. Which New Year do you think sounds the best? Why?
6. Make your own paper lantern for the Chinese lantern festival.

REVIEW

Imagine that you are the new Scottish Government Minister for Society. You have to design a campaign to tackle hate. Choose whether to write a speech, design a poster, design a logo and slogan, or draw a story board for a TV advert to launch your campaign.

10 What are prejudice and discrimination?

What are we exploring?

By the end of this section you should be able to:
- ▶ Explain why people are prejudiced
- ▶ Give examples of stereotypes
- ▶ Challenge attitudes of prejudice and discrimination

Two big issues in Scotland that prevent it from being a real multicultural society are closely linked together: prejudice and discrimination.

What is prejudice?

Prejudice is something that affects the judgements we make about others. To be prejudiced is to have an unfair dislike of someone or something. Usually prejudice exists because of ideas we have about a person, or group of people, before we get to know them. For example, someone who thinks that all old people are grumpy and boring or that all teenagers are lazy and moody is prejudiced. They are making judgements about all old people and teenagers without meeting or thinking about individuals.

People who are prejudiced believe that everyone in a specific group is the same and acts the same way. These people will usually focus on the similarities of people and ignore the differences that make people individuals.

Is it right to make judgements about all teenage or all old people?

 Activate your brain cells!

How do you feel when people judge you in the same way as other teenagers or the same way as your brothers or sisters before they have even met you?

What is a stereotype?

Judging people based on the group they belong to is also known as stereotyping. Stereotypes are a part of everyone's lives and can be entertaining. Comedians use stereotypes in their stand-up routines to make people laugh. We all know that the stereotype that all

A stereotypical Scot

Scots wear kilts, carry bagpipes, have ginger hair and chase haggis around the hills is silly and that most people would not take it seriously. However, some stereotypes can be hurtful and even dangerous. When people believe that stereotypes are real and that the ideas within them are what people are really like, they can be the cause of serious social problems. There are lots of groups of people who are regularly subjected to stereotyping, such as women, teenagers, young mothers, disabled people, old people, young black men, Muslims and obese adults.

When people use stereotypes or prejudice to make decisions or to inform their actions, they are guilty of discrimination. Discrimination against people because of their race is called racism.

What is discrimination?

Discrimination can take many different forms – all of them negative and dangerous. In this example we will look at discrimination in school. This is also known as bullying.

Often discrimination will begin with exclusion. To exclude someone or a group of people is to leave them out, to ignore them. Excluding a person or group of people causes feelings of separation and distance. When people feel excluded they have no sense of belonging and so do not have any feeling of community or loyalty. Think of a person who is being bullied at school, being ignored and excluded. How would you feel if you were in that position?

The next stage of discrimination is language. People who are bullied at school are often the target of name calling and 'slagging off'. They may have graffiti written about them or be shouted at in the playground and corridors. The same thing happens outside school: people experience racism and may be called names; they may have their property defaced with racist graffiti. Think of a person who is being bullied at school, being shouted at and

called names. How would you feel in their position?

The third stage of discrimination is physical. People who are the target of discrimination are sometimes violently attacked. In school a person who is being bullied may be kicked or punched. They may end up bruised and bleeding, or worse. Outside of school, there have been a number of high-profile violent attacks as a result of discrimination in recent years. One well-known attack was on teenager Anthony Walker in 2005, a young black boy who was attacked and killed with an ice axe in a racist attack in Merseyside. Think of a person who is being bullied at school, being tripped up or shoved. How would you feel if that was you?

Show your understanding

1. What is prejudice? Give an example of prejudice that you have seen or heard.
2. What do you think can be done about prejudice?
3. What is a stereotype?
4. Draw a picture of a stereotypical teenager.
5. Discuss your drawing with a partner. Are your drawings negative or positive stereotypes?
6. What is discrimination?
7. Design a poster for your local community to encourage people to challenge ideas of prejudice and discrimination.

Stretch yourself

Does your school have a problem with prejudice or discrimination? Think of ideas for how to tackle prejudice and discrimination in Scottish schools.

REVIEW How do prejudice and discrimination prevent Scotland from being a true multicultural society?

11 Who suffers from prejudice and discrimination in Britain?

What are we exploring?

By the end of this section you should be able to:

▶ Describe discrimination in Britain and give examples
▶ Understand that discrimination can change over time
▶ Recognise that challenging discrimination can result in positive changes

One group of people who have been the subject of race discrimination for centuries is people of mixed-race ethnic origin. People who have parents from two different races have historically been viewed as 'sell-outs' – second-class citizens. They are often the subject of the worst racial abuse because they are seen to be mixing races.

In Britain up until 2001 there was no mixed-race category on census forms. People who were born in Britain to parents from different ethnic groups had to choose which 'side' they belonged to.

Today there are genetic arguments that claim people from mixed-race backgrounds have biological advantages. Because of the wider variety of genes to draw from, people of mixed-race origin may be more talented, fitter, healthier and more intelligent.

When Barack Obama was sworn in as President of the USA on 20 January 2009 it meant a lot of things to a lot of people but perhaps especially to those of mixed-race origin. It was a major victory in the battle against discrimination.

Activate your brain cells!

How would you feel if you had to fill in a census form that did not include your ethnic group?

A man with both a black and a white parent was now one of the most powerful men in the world.

President Obama has made it clear that he is proud of his mixed-race background and yet the media continue to class him as 'black'.

In the last decade attitudes in Britain have begun to change. President Obama is not the only person of mixed-race origin to become successful. There are many celebrities from Britain who are proud of their mixed-race background: Lewis

Barrack Obama and his family

Hamilton on the Grand Prix circuit; Rio Ferdinand and Theo Walcott on the football pitch and Danny Cipriani on the rugby field; Halle Berry in the movies and Mylene Klass on television; Ms Dynamite, Leona Lewis and Alesha Dixon in the music world.

Alesha Dixon grew up in Hertfordshire in England with her white British mother and black Jamaican father. She always felt different because her brothers and sisters were either black or white. She was told early on in her career by record companies that she would never make it in the music industry because she was of mixed-race origin. She is an example of what can happen when people ignore racist discriminatory attitudes. She is proud to be of mixed race and thinks that the media are wrong to report on Barack Obama as a black man because it ignores his white heritage, of which he is equally proud.

The mixed-race ethnic minority is now the fastest growing ethnic group in Britain. Estimates suggest that by 2020 there will be 1.24 million mixed-race people, making it the largest ethnic minority group in Britain. One in ten children now lives in a mixed-race family. This suggests that when views and attitudes are challenged things can change and discrimination can be overcome.

Alesha Dixon

Lewis Hamilton

 Collect a skill

Support a point of view!
Provide evidence to support the idea that people from mixed-race ethnic groups were not recognised in Britain until 2001.

Provide evidence to support the view that being of mixed race in Britain is now more widely accepted.

? Bore your friends...

Alesha Dixon's first job was at Ladbrokes.

 Show your understanding

1. What arguments are there today in favour of mixed-race backgrounds?
2. Why was the election of Barack Obama as President of the USA a big deal?
3. Name four famous British people of mixed-race background.
4. Is Alesha Dixon embarrassed to be from a mixed-race family?

12 What is happening in Turkey?

By the end of this section you should be able to:

▶ Explain why Turkey is an interesting country to study

▶ Give an example of a human rights issue in Turkey

▶ Describe how government decisions have an impact on people's lives

Turkey is a country that sits right on the border between the East and the West.

This means that it is torn between two different histories, **cultures** and **values**. It contains a unique blend of Eastern and Western traditions.

Cultures ideas, customs and art of a particular society/ group of people.

Values principles or beliefs. Something that a person thinks is important.

Activate your brain cells!

Close your eyes and try to picture the difference between Eastern and Western culture.

What does that mean?

The West refers to countries that can trace their people to mainly western European countries. These are mainly Christian countries. The East refers to countries that have evolved separately from European influence. These countries have many different religions: for example, Buddhism, Judaism, Taoism and Islam. Eastern and Western values often clash. This means that Turkey is a country where conflicts can occur between different groups.

What is the problem?

The **constitution** of Turkey is **secular**. This is because Turkey became a republic in 1923 and was made up of lots of different communities of people. To stop people fighting about which religion the country should follow, Mustafa Atatürk (Turkey's first President) made Turkey a secular society.

Constitution the rules by which a country is run.

Secular without religion.

The problem is that as a part of the constitution, religious symbols are banned from government buildings. This means that girls who believe they should wear headscarves as part of their religion are not allowed to do so at university or college. They feel their right to an education is being taken away from them because their religious beliefs mean they cannot remove the scarf. Some girls have gone as far as to buy wigs and wear them on top of their scarves in order to defend their beliefs.

12

Where else in the world do people face discrimination and prejudice?

What has the government done about it?

In February 2008 Turkey passed changes to the law to ease the ban on headscarves in universities. Some people in Turkey believe that this is a problem because it is allowing **Islamic** religious beliefs to affect decisions.

Islamic culture relating to Muslim religion.

Other people believe that the ban is preventing these girls from their basic right to Higher Education. They say the scarf is an expression of their personal religious beliefs and that it is their right to choose how to dress.

Turkey's population is mostly Muslim, so 65 per cent of all Turkish women cover their heads. This means that thousands of girls have been missing out on the opportunity to attend college and university.

On the other hand there are also tens of thousands of people who are against the change and they have held many protest rallies to put across their point.

These people believe that Turkey must remain a secular society and that allowing the change could lead to too much Islamic influence on their government.

 ### Show your understanding

1. Why does Turkey's geography make it an interesting country to study?
2. Turkey has a secular constitution. What does this mean?
3. Why does the constitution cause problems for some girls in Turkey?
4. What have some girls chosen to do as a result?
5. Do you think that the headscarf ban breaches human rights?
6. Think about how you would feel if it were you, or your sister, who was not allowed to wear a headscarf. Write a letter to Human Rights Watch or design a leaflet to raise awareness of the issue.

Stretch yourself

Think about what is going on in Turkey and then think about the government in this country. The way a government runs a country can have good and bad effects on the people who live there. Discuss this with a partner and make a list of good effects and bad effects that governments can have on their people.

REVIEW Think again about the difference between Eastern and Western culture. Draw two pictures – one to symbolise Eastern culture and one to symbolise Western culture.

13 What is happening in Afghanistan?

What are we exploring?

By the end of this section you should be able to:

▶ Explain why Afghanistan is a poor country
▶ Describe how people's lives are affected by government

Why study Afghanistan?

Afghanistan is a country that has had a troubled time in recent history. It has a population of around 28 million and in 2008 20 million of them were estimated to be living in poverty. This makes Afghanistan one of the poorest countries in the world. The country's infrastructure has been heavily damaged by decades of fighting, and life expectancy is only 44 years for men and women.

Afghanistan is a landlocked country in an important geographical position between the Middle East, Central Asia and India. It has been fought over throughout history.

The Taliban, a group of Islamic students, came to power in 1996 and brought stability in a country where civil war raged for a long time.

What was life like under the Taliban?

Life in Afghanistan during the rule of the Taliban was extremely strict, especially for women. The Taliban are a lot more extreme than most Muslims. Afghan women and girls faced discrimination in almost every aspect of their lives. Women were not allowed out in public alone under any circumstances. Even when they did leave the home they had to ensure they always wore a burka, which covers their entire face and body, leaving only a mesh to see through. The Taliban wanted to turn Afghanistan into the purest Muslim country in the world.

Things banned under the Taliban		
movies	the Internet	non-religious music
musical instruments	dancing	photographs of people and animals
fireworks	kite-flying	playing cards
chess	soft toys	make-up
fashion magazines	women going out on their own	education for girls

What happened to the Taliban?

When the Taliban controlled Afghanistan, they allowed a terrorist group called Al Qaeda to have bases in the country. In September 2001, thousands were killed in the 9/11 terrorist attacks in New York and Washington. The United States believe that Osama Bin Laden (the leader of Al Qaeda) was the man behind these attacks. The Taliban refused to hand over Osama Bin Laden to the Americans so in October 2001 the USA began bombing the Taliban and the members of Al Qaeda in Afghanistan.

This gave the people in Afghanistan who had opposed the Taliban the motivation to stand up for themselves, and by December 2001 the Taliban had fallen from power.

13

Where else in the world do people face discrimination and prejudice?

Activate your brain cells!

Can you imagine life without the things that the Taliban banned? Make a list in your jotter of feelings you may experience if all of those things were banned in this country.

Collect a skill

Calculating percentages!

What is the percentage of Afghanistan's population who live in poverty?

(Remember, to calculate a percentage: smaller number/larger number x 100)

Are things any better in Afghanistan now?

The situation in Afghanistan just now is still very difficult for the people. There has been a lot of fighting as the Taliban try to regain power. The new Afghan government and the authorities are strong in the capital city of Kabul but they have little control outside of the city.

Women and girls still face discrimination in all aspects of their lives. Most girls have never been enrolled in school: 37 per cent of primary school pupils are girls and only 27 per cent in secondary schools.

Another barrier for girls is that they have to travel long distances to reach mixed or girls-only schools. On the journey to school girls face sexual harassment, violence and abduction. A dramatic increase in the number of women teachers is needed, as almost half the districts in the country do not have a single female teacher.

Almost 60 per cent of girls in Afghanistan are married before they reach sixteen years of age. The legal age of marriage is sixteen for females and eighteen for males but this doesn't stop the practice of child marriage from continuing. Child marriage is a major threat to girls' health. Teenage pregnancy is one of the main causes of death in childbirth in the country.

There are some changes and hope for women in Afghanistan. Women trying to escape forced or violent marriages in Kabul and other cities can now turn to charities and support organisations. However, in rural areas things are slow to change. International pressure groups like Human Rights Watch and Amnesty International continue to put pressure on the USA and the rest of the world to help the people of Afghanistan.

Show your understanding

1. Who are the Taliban?
2. Draw a spider diagram to show things banned by the Taliban when they were in power in Afghanistan.
3. How did the Taliban's rule end?
4. Provide evidence to show that life in Afghanistan is still very hard.
5. Design a campaign poster to draw attention to the problems faced by women in Afghanistan.

Learning link

Does anyone fight for human rights?

REVIEW Think about what is going on in Afghanistan. Many people in Britain think that our soldiers should not be working in Afghanistan and that the troops should be recalled. Do you think that the people of Afghanistan need help to rebuild their country or should they be left alone to sort out the problems?

14 What is democracy?

What are we exploring?

By the end of this section you should be able to:

▶ Explain what democracy is

▶ Explain how democracy works

▶ Explain why voting is important

Democracy is a political system that allows everyone to have a say in how the country is run. People's rights are very important in a democracy – for example, the right to vote and speak out against the government.

Activate your brain cells!

Think about it! What makes democracy a good political system?

How does democracy work?

Democracy comes from Ancient Greece. The word originally comes from two Greek words demos (people) and kratos (rule): rule by the people. More than 2500 years ago, in the city of Athens, all male citizens voted on all decisions of government. This was called direct democracy.

Obviously, this would not work in modern Scotland. There are 5.2 million people in Scotland. If everyone tried to have their say directly, it would be very noisy and decisions would take a long time. Imagine if everyone in your class tried to give their opinion at the same time and then multiply the noise and confusion by 173,000. This is why we have elections to elect **representatives** who speak on our behalf. They represent us in Parliament. This is called representative democracy. Lots of countries today are representative democracies: for example, France, Germany and the United States of America.

Representative a person who speaks on behalf of others.

So can everyone vote?

No. There are several people who are not allowed to vote. You are not allowed to vote until you are eighteen years of age. People who have been convicted of a crime lose their right to vote while they are in prison. Members of the House of Lords are not allowed to vote. People with learning disabilities or mental illness who are not able to make a rational decision are not allowed to vote. Members of the Royal family are allowed to vote but choose not to do so.

Everyone else who is over eighteen, a citizen of the United Kingdom and registered on the **Electoral Register** is allowed to vote.

Electoral Register the list of all the people who are allowed to vote.

Collect a skill

Discussion!

People in prison are not allowed to vote. Do you think that this is fair? Make a list of reasons for your answer that you could use in a class discussion.

Remember the most important rule for successful class discussion is to listen! Never interrupt and always think carefully about what your classmates are saying before responding.

Was this always the case?

No. When democracy began in Britain only men who owned land were allowed to vote. Throughout the 1800s the right to vote was gradually given to more and more men but still women were not allowed to vote. A group of women were not happy about this and fought hard for the right to vote. They were known as the Suffragettes. Women first gained the vote in 1918 but did not achieve equal voting rights with men until 1928.

One Suffragette called Emily Davison was famous because she died when she stepped out in front of the King's horse at the Epsom Derby in 1913. The Suffragettes were an early example of a group of people who took direct action to try to influence those in power – a pressure group. Many of the Suffragettes were arrested for violent behaviour and staged hunger strikes while in jail. Davison even went as far as to plant a bomb at the newly built home of David Lloyd George, the Chancellor of the Exchequer, damaging it severely. She also hid in a cupboard in the Houses of Parliament on the night of the 1911 census so that she could officially state her place of residence as the House of Commons.

The fact that so many people fought so hard for the right to vote is one of the reasons why it is so important and why everyone should use their right.

Show your understanding

1. What does democracy mean?
2. How did direct democracy work?
3. Why would direct democracy not work today?
4. How does representative democracy work?
5. 'Everyone over 18 in Britain can vote.' This is the view of Neil Patrick. Do you agree with Neil Patrick? Give reasons for your answer.
6. Have women always been allowed to vote?
7. What do you think of Emily Davison? Give reasons for your answer.

REVIEW

Why is it important to vote?

? Bore your friends ...

New Zealand was the first self-governing country in the world to grant women the vote. In 1893, all women over the age of 21 were permitted to vote in parliamentary elections.

15 Who represents me?

What are we exploring?

By the end of this section you should be able to:

▶ Describe how representation works

▶ Give examples of the people who represent you

▶ Summarise information in a factfile

There are lots of different people who represent us at different levels. On the smallest level your parents represent you and make decisions for you: for example, where you live, what time you go to bed and where you go to school. Your teachers and head teacher also represent you and make decisions for you: for example, which subjects you learn and the length of your lessons.

When you go higher than this, the people who represent you are elected. This means that an election is held and adults aged eighteen and over are allowed to vote for the people they think will do the best job.

Local councillors

On a local level we are represented by local councillors. These people work on our behalf to make decisions about local services. They are elected every four years. There are 32 councils in Scotland and each one has councillors to meet their needs and make decisions at a local level. The number of councillors varies: East Lothian has 23 councillors, Glasgow has 79 and Highland has 80 councillors.

Local councillors represent us by looking after our local services, such as education, housing, roads, leisure facilities and refuse collection. Local councils are effective because councillors live in the local area and use the services themselves, so they know what works and what doesn't work.

 Activate your brain cells!

Think about the people who represent you (make decisions for you). Make a list of as many as you can.

Members of the Scottish Parliament (MSPs)

At the next level are the people who represent us in Scotland as a whole. These people are called MSPs. They are elected every four years to make decisions for us about Scottish issues, such as health care, education, crime and the environment.

MSPs work in the Scottish Parliament in Edinburgh for three days a week and at home in their local constituency for two days a week.

Learning link

What happens in the Scottish Parliament?

Members of Parliament (MPs)

The next level is the United Kingdom. Here our representatives are called MPs.

They are elected at least every five years. MPs work in the Houses of Parliament in Westminster in London. There are two houses in Westminster: the House of Commons and the House of Lords. MPs work in the House of Commons. MPs represent us in decision making on UK issues such as national security, defence, foreign affairs and drugs.

There are 59 Scottish MPs at Westminster to represent Scotland's point of view on these UK issues. The total number of MPs is 646.

Members of the European Parliament (MEPs)

The next level up is Europe. The United Kingdom is a member of the European Union. This means that we also elect people to represent us at European level. MEPs make decisions for us about European issues such as climate change, food safety and quality, and travel. There are seven MEPs to represent the interests of Scotland in Europe. The total number of MEPs is 785. They are elected every five years.

Show your understanding

1. In what ways do your parents represent you?
2. How are the people who represent you chosen?
3. For each of the four representatives in the text make a factfile that includes the following information: title, level, how often are they elected, how many are there, what do they make decisions about?

16 What is an election campaign?

By the end of this section you should be able to:

▶ Explain what an election campaign is

▶ Explain how people can participate in election campaigns

📁 Collect a skill

Boost your word power!

Remember to use the vocabulary bubbles to help you learn new words and boost your word power.

In the run-up to an election the **candidates** and political parties try to get the voters' attention. Each one tries to persuade people to vote for them. This is called the election campaign. It provides lots of opportunities for people to get involved and participate in politics.

> **Candidates** people who are standing in the election and want to be representatives.

What can people do?

Anyone can join a political party and help them with their campaign. There are many different methods that parties use when campaigning.

1. **Put up posters**
   Positives: bright; eye-catching; can be displayed all over the constituency; a small amount of wording allows parties to highlight their key **policies**.
   Negatives: other parties can paste their posters over the top; posters can become litter after the election.

> **Policies** promises political parties make about what they will do if they win an election.

2. **Hand out balloons, stickers and rosettes**
   Positives: bright; eye-catching; will be seen by others in the street.
   Negatives: no space to explain policies; can become litter if people are not interested.

3. **Hand out leaflets and distribute leaflets to people's homes**
   Positives: lots of room to explain policies in detail; can make sure everyone sees them by posting them through every household door.
   Negatives: people might just put them in the bin without reading them; expensive; not very environmentally friendly.

4. **Talk to voters about the issues (in public and by visiting them at home)**
   Positives: candidates can answer questions in detail; voters can get to know the candidates and might be more likely to vote for them.
   Negatives: candidates can't get around every village and town in their **constituency** and this is very time-consuming.

> **Constituency** the area a representative will speak on behalf of in Parliament.

5. Appear on TV and Radio

Positives: can reach a large number of people; can explain policies in detail; can show personality and try to convince voters to like him/her.

Negatives: difficult to get TV and radio interviews unless the candidate is the party leader.

6. Party Political Broadcasts

Positives: by law each of the main parties must be given the same amount of time on TV; broadcasts are like adverts and so can show in detail all the best bits of the party and their policies.

Negatives: limited amount of time; only show the party and leader, not the other constituency candidates.

7. Make speeches and attend public meetings

Positives: can meet voters in large numbers and show personality; can explain policies in detail.

Negatives: voters might not turn up to listen; those who do are likely to vote for the candidate anyway so it doesn't win any new votes.

8. Use cars with loudspeakers to repeatedly broadcast the party's policies

Positives: can reach lots of voters and explain policies in detail.

Negatives: can be very annoying; voters only hear part of the policy before the car drives on.

9. Give newspaper interviews

Positives: can reach large numbers of voters; takes a short amount of time.

Negatives: journalists can twist what the candidate says or may only print part of what they say.

10. Use websites and online adverts

Positives: cheap; bright; eye-catching; can be as detailed as the candidate wants.

Negatives: will only be seen by those who use the Internet regularly and who visit those websites.

Show your understanding

1. What is a candidate?
2. What is an election campaign?
3. Why do political parties and candidates need voters' attention?
4. How can people participate in an election campaign?
5. Choose three methods used during an election campaign and give an advantage and disadvantage of each.
6. What is a policy?

Stretch yourself

Now you have the opportunity to campaign for yourself. Choose any of the methods and imagine that you are the candidate. Either design a poster or leaflet or write a speech. Remember you will need a colour and a name for your political party.

REVIEW

Imagine your friend texts you the night before a test to say she does not understand what an election campaign is. Write a reply text message of less than 160 characters.

17 Who are the main political parties?

What are we exploring?

By the end of this section you should be able to:

▶ Discuss the four main political parties

▶ Explain what a political party is

In Scotland there are four main political parties: Scottish National Party (SNP), Labour, Conservative and Liberal Democrat. A political party is an organisation made up of people who share similar political beliefs and who wish to influence the running of a country through an elected parliament.

 Activate your brain cells!

Think about it! Why do politicians want to belong to political parties?

FACTFILE: The Scottish National Party

The Scottish National Party has yellow as its colour. It is the only party to have the same leader at Holyrood and Westminster, Alex Salmond. Alex Salmond is the First Minister of Scotland and the SNP is the party in power in Scotland.

Three SNP policies are:

- To make Scotland the world leader in wave and tidal power.
- High-speed rail link between London and Scotland.
- Increased sentences for knife crime.

This is the party symbol:

FACTFILE: The Labour Party

The Labour Party has red as its colour. The leader in Scotland is Iain Gray. Following the May 2010 election Gordon Brown resigned as UK leader. A leadership contest will decide who will be the new leader of the party.

Three Labour Party policies are:

- Create 400,000 new green jobs by 2015.
- 15 hours a week of free nursery education for three and four year olds.
- A free vote in Parliament on reducing the voting age to sixteen.

Leader until 2010

This is the party symbol:

FACTFILE: The Conservative Party

The Conservative Party has blue as its colour. The leader in Scotland is Annabelle Goldie and the UK leader is David Cameron. David Cameron is the Prime Minister because the Conservative Party and the Liberal Democrats joined together after the 2010 election to form a **coalition** and take power in Westminster.

Three Conservative Party policies are:

- Develop high-speed rail network connecting cities in Scotland, England and Wales.
- Allow parents to share maternity leave.
- Strengthen the police powers of stop and search.

This is the party symbol:

FACTFILE: The Liberal Democrat Party

The Liberal Democrat Party has gold as its colour. The leader in Scotland is Tavish Scott and the UK leader is Nick Clegg. Nick Clegg is the Deputy Prime Minister at Westminster after the Liberal Democrat formed a coalition government with the Conservatives in May 2010.

Three Liberal Democrat Party policies are:

- Increase police numbers.
- Investment in a UK-wide high-speed rail network.
- No nuclear power stations.

This is the party symbol:

 Show your understanding

1. What is a political party?
2. Who are the four main political parties in Scotland?
3. Who are the leaders of the four parties?
4. Draw the symbols of the four main parties.
5. Choose one policy from each party and explain why you think it is important.
6. Which party would you vote for if you were eighteen? Give reasons for your answer.

Coalition when two or more parties join together to form a government.

Stretch yourself

An important part of a political party's identity is its colour and symbol. Imagine you are creating a new political party. Design a symbol for the party.

18 How do elections work?

Elections are a key part of democracy in Britain; they allow people the chance to choose who they want to represent them. Polling day finally arrives after weeks of campaigning and people can vote for their representatives.

Activate your brain cells!

Think about what happens when people vote. Why is it important that people can vote in secret?

How do people vote?

Look at the Polling station walkthrough at http://www.aboutmyvote.co.uk/how_do_i_vote/polling_station_walkthrough.aspx

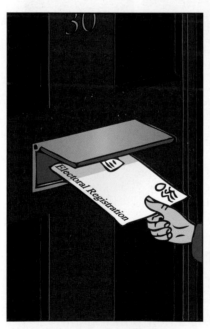

Step 1: To be eligible to vote you must be registered on the Electoral Register. Once a year, a form is sent through the post to every household asking who is living there. Once you turn seventeen you will be placed on the form so that you are immediately able to vote when you turn eighteen.

Step 2: In the run-up to an election, a polling card will come through the post. This tells you where to vote and when. Your local polling station will usually be a community hall or primary school. It will be open from 7am to 10pm on the day of the election.

Step 3: On the day of the election you take the polling card to the polling station and a clerk will check your name and address on the register. The clerk does this to make sure that you have not already voted. They will then give you a ballot paper.

Step 4: You take your ballot paper to one of the polling booths. This shelters you so that you can vote in secret. In a UK election you must put a X beside the candidate you want to win.

Step 5: You must then fold your ballot paper in half and place it in the ballot box. You have now placed your vote! At the end of the day all of the ballot boxes will be collected and taken to a central place to be counted. You can watch the news to find out who has won!

Collect a skill

Boost your word power!

Match up these heads and tails.

Ballot box	You mark your vote on it.
Electoral Register	It comes through your door and tells you where and when to vote.
Ballot paper	You put your vote in it.
Polling station	A list of everyone who is eligible to vote.
Polling card	This is where you go to vote.

 Show your understanding

1. What name is given to the day when people vote in an election?
2. What do you have to do so that you are eligible to vote?
3. Where do you go to vote?
4. Why does the clerk check your name against the register? Do you think that this is important?
5. The following sequence has been messed up. Put the sketches in the correct order and write the letter in your jotter.

19 What can people do?

By the end of this section you should be able to:

▶ Explain what a pressure group is

▶ Describe the methods used by pressure groups

▶ Give examples of pressure groups

Besides standing as a candidate and helping with an election campaign, there are lots of other ways that people in Scotland can influence the people in power and the decisions they make. Two of the main areas of influence are:

• Pressure groups

• The media

What are pressure groups?

A pressure group is an organisation that does not want to become the government but wants to influence the government's decisions.

 Activate your brain cells!

Think about pressure groups. Do you think they are important? Why or why not?

People used to join a political party when they wanted to have their say in how the government ran the country. Today people are more likely to join a pressure group in order to influence the government. There are only a few political parties, such as the Labour Party, the Conservative Party, the Liberal Democrats and the SNP, but there are thousands of pressure groups.

Pressure groups allow people to influence decisions and get involved with politics in between elections. Sometimes they can make a difference. For example, the pressure group SKAT (Skye and Kyle

Against Tolls) claims to have been one of the key forces behind the government's decision to remove the tolls from the Skye Road Bridge.

What do pressure groups do?

Pressure groups use lots of different methods to influence the government.

One of the first ways pressure groups can do this is by telling the people who make the laws (the Scottish Parliament) what they would like changed. Some pressure groups try to speed up change by working with the government to write laws and make changes. Most pressure groups try to put pressure on the government by carrying out actions to get noticed by the public and by the media.

What is a petition and how does it work?

A petition is a request for action. Any individual or group can petition the Scottish Parliament to find out about an issue or concern, change a law, or introduce a new law.

The Scottish Parliament has a Public Petitions Committee. This means that there is a group of MSPs who have to read every petition submitted to the Scottish Parliament, even the ones with only one signature. Anyone can submit a petition about something they care about, even you. Since the Parliament opened in 1999 it has received over 1,000 petitions. The image below shows pupils from All Saints Secondary School in Glasgow presenting the

1,000th petition to the Parliament. The petition asked the government to consider the public health impact of cheaply available alcohol.

In March 2009 the Committee went to Fraserburgh Academy in Aberdeenshire to hear from pupils who had petitioned the Parliament about local healthcare provision in rural areas and on poverty and deprivation in Africa.

Pressure groups often use a petition to get the attention of those in power and to ask them to solve a problem or change something. For example, the group Epilepsy Scotland petitioned the Parliament in 2009 to increase the number of epilepsy specialist nurses.

What else do pressure groups do?

Groups can protest in lots of different ways. Plane Stupid is a pressure group that wants to raise awareness about climate change and let the public know about the damage caused by increasing numbers of flights. In March 2009 they disrupted flights at Aberdeen airport. Protesters camped out on the runway in a 'wire fortress' and climbed on the roof of the airport with a banner. Four flights were cancelled and several were delayed. The protesters said that their campaign was to raise awareness of the growing impact of air travel on climate change.

Activities like the ones carried out by Plane Stupid are illegal and the protesters often get arrested. People do these things to try to get media attention for their cause.

Collect a skill

Identify exaggeration!

> *Only members of pressure groups can submit petitions to the Scottish Parliament.*

This is the view of Robert Hamilton. Can Robert Hamilton be accused of exaggeration? Give reasons to support your answer.

Show your understanding

1. What is a pressure group?
2. Why are pressure groups important?
3. Give an example of a pressure group that has made a difference.
4. Why do some pressure groups work with the government?
5. Give two examples of petitions submitted to the Scottish Parliament.
6. Are all pressure group methods legal? Give reasons to support your answer.

Stretch yourself

Think about things that are important to you.

If you were to form a pressure group what would you want to change? Make up a name for your pressure group and design a logo.

20 Who are the Gurkhas?

What are we exploring?

By the end of this section you should be able to:

▶ Give a detailed example of a successful pressure group

▶ Discuss celebrity involvement in pressure groups

▶ Use the Internet to find out more about the Gurkhas

For almost 200 years the Gurkhas have fought as a part of the British Army. During the time of the British Empire the Gurkhas were recognised as being a strong and brave race of natural fighters. The Nepalese Gurkha soldiers have the motto 'Better to die than be a coward.'

In 1815, the British East India Company lost many men when trying to invade Nepal. They signed a peace deal that allowed them to recruit soldiers from their enemy: the Gurkhas. Throughout both World Wars the Gurkhas fought and died for the British Army. Then, when India gained independence from Britain in 1947, an agreement was signed between Nepal, India and Britain. Six regiments were transferred to the new Indian Army and four to the British Army.

The Gurkhas have continued to fight for the British Army up to the present day and have recently been serving in Iraq and Afghanistan.

What is the problem?

The problem is that after the Gurkhas have served their time in the army (a minimum of fifteen years to secure a pension) they are discharged back to Nepal. Historically, they received a much smaller pension – at least six times less – than British soldiers. This was justified because the cost of living is much lower in Nepal than in Britain. However, many Gurkhas have wished to remain in Britain and they do not have enough money to survive. In March 2007 the government announced that all Gurkhas who retired after 1997 would be granted the same pension as the rest of the army.

Why are people still campaigning for their rights?

Gurkhas who retired after 1997 have automatic permission to remain in Britain but those who retired before then have to apply and may be refused and deported. Since September 2008 there have been many protests for the rights of the Gurkhas. Actress Joanna Lumley has helped raise awareness for the Gurkhas' campaign because her father served with the Gurkhas.

input in the formation of new laws. Shortly after this, Gordon Brown was defeated in the House of Commons as MPs voted to allow all Gurkhas who had retired before 1997 and who had completed at least four years of service, to settle permanently in the UK. This shows how much power Joanna Lumley has been able to bring to the campaign.

Sometimes pressure groups can try to recruit celebrities to their cause because this helps them to get the public's attention and also keeps the media interested. Joanna Lumley has run a very clever campaign for the Gurkhas, using every connection she has in order to raise awareness and make the government listen.

In May 2009, Ms Lumley arranged an on-the-spot press conference with the government minister in charge of immigration. She told him that the rejection of five Gurkha appeals was 'shocking'. The minister indicated that campaigners would be allowed to have an

In July 2009 Ms Lumley made a trip to Nepal to meet with the Prime Minister and President. She was greeted by crowds of people with signs describing her as a 'goddess'. The people of Nepal wanted to thank her for her part in the campaign.

Stretch yourself

Use a search engine, such as Google™, to try to find other examples of pressure groups that have used celebrities to get attention for their cause.

 Show your understanding

1. What is the Gurkhas' motto?
2. Why do the Gurkhas fight for the British Army?
3. Why might people think that the way the Gurkhas were treated when they retired before 1997 was unfair?
4. How did Britain justify this?
5. Why is Joanna Lumley involved in the campaign?

REVIEW

Do you think that having celebrities involved with a campaign is a good idea? Discuss with a partner. Give reasons to support your answer.

❓ Bore your friends...

The Sherpa of Nepal believe that the Abominable Snowman lives in the high snow-covered mountains but it has never been discovered.

21 How do the media influence people?

What are we exploring?

By the end of this section you should be able to:
▶ Explain what the three main types of media are
▶ Identify bias

There are three main types of news media in modern society: print media (newspapers and magazines), broadcast media (television and radio) and electronic media (the Internet). Through the media we receive information about politics, successes, disasters and accidents, world issues and crimes.

 Activate your brain cells!

Discuss with a partner: Why do we need media?

Television and radio must be impartial. There are laws to control what can and cannot be broadcast. This means they must always show both sides of a story and cannot tell the story to make one group or person sound better than the other.

Newspapers and magazines are allowed to and often do show political bias. For example, *The Daily Mail* and *The Daily* *Telegraph* tend to support the Conservative Party while *The Daily Record* and *The Herald* support the Labour Party. *The Sun* supported the Labour Party for the 1997 election but currently supports the Conservative Party.

The Internet is often referred to as 'the new media'. Most major print and television media now have online sites where people can access news stories at any time of the day or night. Anyone can publish something on the Internet and stories can be made available instantly across the world. The fact that anyone can post stories means that we must be very careful when using information from the Internet.

Sometimes newspapers can organise campaigns and actively support a pressure group. One example of this is the campaign run by Andrew Morton's parents to get all airguns banned in Scotland. Andrew Morton was killed, aged two, in Easterhouse, Glasgow. He was shot in the head with an airgun while watching fire engines near his home.

 **Collect a skill**

What is bias and exaggeration?

Learning new skills is an important part of studying Modern Studies. One key skill is to be able to identify bias and exaggeration. Bias means to support or oppose a particular person or thing in an unfair way by allowing personal opinions to influence your judgement. Exaggeration means making something seem larger, more important, better, or worse than it really is.

Newspapers and magazines are owned by private companies and so they can be biased in the way they report stories. Below are two newspaper stories reporting on the same event.

1. What is bias?
2. Read the two newspaper articles about the opening of the new National Stadium. Which one could be accused of being biased in favour of the First Minister?
3. Give an example of a word or phrase from the other newspaper that shows it is biased against the First Minister.

The Voice

First Minister delivers brilliant speech at National Stadium opening

The First Minister yesterday delivered a brilliant speech at the opening of the fantastic new National Stadium. The sports stadium in Edinburgh was built thanks to an increase in funding for sports from the First Minister's party. It represents the overall success of the Government over the last four years: more police officers on the street, student debt has been reduced, more schools have been built and class sizes are shrinking. An excellent speech from a strong leader.

The Witness

First Minister again fails to deliver the goods at stadium opening

The First Minister failed to inspire at yesterday's poorly attended National Stadium opening. His speech was as poor quality as the stadium itself which does not meet the standard expected. He failed to provide many positive examples of what has been achieved by his Government in the last four years. Crime is on the increase and teachers are struggling to find work. A further disappointment from the weak leader of the Government.

 Show your understanding

1. What are the three main types of media?
2. What is the function of the media?
3. Why do you think politicians prefer broadcast media to print media?
4. Give examples of newspapers that are biased towards one of the political parties.
5. Why should you be careful about information taken from the Internet?

Stretch yourself

Write a paragraph describing something that has happened to you recently. It could be about a sports game, a school event or something you have seen on the TV. Make sure your paragraph describes the event in a biased way.

? Bore your friends ...

'Oor Wullie' first appeared in The Sunday Post newspaper on 8 March 1936.

22 What is the difference between Holyrood and Westminster?

What are we exploring?

By the end of this section you should be able to:

▶ Explain key differences between Holyrood and Westminster

▶ Give examples of reserved and devolved matters

📁 Collect a skill

Boost your word power!

There are so many different words that are used when studying politics and democracy that it can all become very confusing. A group of words that relates to a specific topic or subject is called terminology. So words relating to politics are called political terminology. Don't forget to use the glossary boxes to help you learn new words and boost your word power.

One important distinction that all students need to understand is the difference between Holyrood and Westminster.

Holyrood is the name given to the Scottish Parliament because it is built in the Holyrood area of Edinburgh. The UK Parliament is housed in London in the Palace of Westminster. There are many differences between the two parliaments including their areas of power.

In 1997 the Scottish people were given the chance to vote in a **referendum** to decide whether or not Scotland should have its own Parliament. They were also asked whether or not the Parliament should have tax-varying powers. On the day of the referendum 60.4 per cent of the **electorate** turned out to vote and the answer was yes to both questions. On 1 July 1999 the Scottish Parliament was officially opened by the Queen.

> **Referendum** a vote in which the people are asked to give their opinion or answer a question.

> **Electorate** all the people in a country who are eligible to vote and are registered to vote.

Activate your brain cells!

If you had been eighteen in 1997 how would you have voted in the referendum? Why?

Because Scotland is not an independent country, Holyrood is home to a devolved government. This means that the UK Parliament has handed down some powers to the Scottish Parliament and allows them to make decisions on these issues. The issues which have been handed down to Scotland are called devolved matters. The table opposite shows some of the matters which are devolved to Scotland.

The Scottish Parliament at Holyrood is very different from the UK Parliament. The building of the Scottish Parliament is new. It was completed in 2004 and was extremely controversial. The final cost of the building was £414.4 million but the original amount of money estimated for the building was £40 million. This was not a good start for the Scottish Parliament and many people thought that it was a sign that Scotland could not handle having its own powers.

Collect a skill

Identify bias!

The Scottish Parliament building is a brilliant symbol of Scotland.

This is the view of Sarah MacIntosh. Do you think that Sarah's view is biased? Give reasons to support your answer.

Westminster has been home to decision-making powers for over 900 years. The Palace of Westminster contains the two Houses of Parliament: the House of Commons and the House of Lords.

The House of Commons is the main house. This is where MPs from Scotland, England,

Wales and Northern Ireland represent the people of the United Kingdom. The House of Commons makes decisions and passes laws on issues that have not been devolved to Scotland, Wales or Northern Ireland. These issues are known as reserved issues. Some of these are shown in the table below.

The House of Lords has approximately 720 members, known as peers. The House of Lords is the second house of the Houses of Parliament. This means it does not have as much power as the House of Commons but it can amend bills and delay them from becoming law.

Devolved matters	Reserved matters
Health	Defence
Local government	Equal opportunities
Housing	Guns and weapons
Tourism	National security
Police and fire services	Trade and industry
Education	Abortion
Social work	Broadcasting/entertainment
Environment	Drug laws

Show your understanding

1. What is the name given to a group of words relating to a topic?
2. Why are the Scottish and UK Parliaments called Holyrood and Westminster?
3. What is a referendum?
4. How did Scotland get its own parliament?
5. What does 'devolved government' mean?
6. Why was the building of the Scottish Parliament controversial?
7. List three differences between Holyrood and Westminster.
8. What is the difference between reserved and devolved matters? Give examples in your answer.

Bore your friends ...

The clock on the tower of Big Ben in London slowed down by 5 minutes in 1949 when a flock of starlings landed on the minute hand.

23 Who's who?

What are we exploring?

By the end of this section you should be able to:
▶ Identify key figures in the Scottish Parliament
▶ Identify key figures in the UK Parliament
▶ Recognise differences between the two parliaments

Holyrood

The **First Minister of Scotland** is the head of the Scottish Parliament. So far this has always been the leader of the largest party after an election but it doesn't have to be. The First Minister is elected by all of the MSPs following an election.

The Clerks are employed by the Parliament. They advise the Presiding Officer.

The Presiding Officer has a very important role in the Scottish Parliament. She or he is elected by all of the MSPs and is responsible for looking after the rights of all MSPs. The Presiding Officer makes sure that debates are fair and that everyone who speaks is given the same time and respect. The Presiding Officer is expected to remain neutral and so must give up their political party. They only vote if there is a tie.

There are 131 seats and desks in the debating chamber for the 129 MSPs and 2 Law Officers.

The Law Officers advise the Parliament on legal matters. They sit in the chamber but are not allowed to vote in the chamber.

Cabinet Secretaries and Government Ministers sit with the First Minister. These are senior members of the winning party that the First Minister has chosen to run each of the Government departments.

MSPs can sit anywhere they like in the chamber but they usually sit in their party groups.

Westminster

The **Prime Minister** is the leader of the party who wins the most seats after a general election. She or he is the leader of the government and will choose senior party members to be their Government Ministers. These Government Ministers sit on the front bench.

The Speaker is in charge of the House of Commons. She or he keeps order in the House and controls the debates. As with the Presiding Officer, the Speaker must give up their political party so that they act impartially. The Speaker is chosen by all of the MPs after a general election.

There are 646 MPs but there is not enough space for them all to sit down in the House of Commons – there are only 427 seats. When an important vote or debate is taking place and the House is full, MPs have to stand along the walls and sit on the steps.

The Leader of the Opposition is the leader of the party who came second in the election. They also choose senior party members to form a Shadow Cabinet. These Shadow Cabinet members sit opposite the government on the front bench.

All other **Members of Parliament** are known as backbenchers because they sit behind the government or shadow ministers.

❓ Bore your friends...

In Belgium 55% of government ministers are female.

Show your understanding

1. Who is the First Minister of Scotland?
2. Where do government ministers sit in Holyrood and in Westminster?
3. Who is the Prime Minister?
4. Why is the Presiding Officer an important role in the Scottish Parliament?
5. Is there a similar role in the UK Parliament? What is it?
6. List three differences between the debating chambers in Holyrood and Westminster.
7. Draw a rough sketch of each of the two parliaments and mark on your sketch where everyone sits.

24 What happens in the Scottish Parliament?

By the end of this section you should be able to:

▶ List the four founding principles of the Scottish Parliament

▶ Explain how the Scottish Parliament works to meet the four founding principles

▶ Describe what happens on different days of the week in the Scottish Parliament

The Scottish Parliament is the place where decisions are made on devolved matters for the people of Scotland.

Learning link

What is the difference between Holyrood and Westminster?

 Activate your brain cells!

Do you think we need a Scottish Parliament? Why or why not?

Four key principles

When the Scottish Parliament was created it was done with four key principles in mind:

- Equal Opportunities
- Access and Participation
- Sharing the Power
- Accountability

Equal opportunities

The Scottish Parliament ensures that it promotes equal opportunities by:

- having family-friendly working hours – decision time is normally at 5pm. This is when MSPs decide on motions and bills that have been discussed that day. In Westminster this does not happen until the debate comes to an end, which can often be late at night

- having designated constituency days on Mondays and Fridays to allow MSPs to be at home with their families at the weekend

- an equal opportunities committee which looks after the interests of all the people of Scotland.

Access and participation

The Scottish Parliament ensures access and participation by:

- allowing the public to attend meetings of the Parliament

- having a dedicated Public Information Service to answer all queries

- updating the website with Parliament documents

- holding public consultations where people can have their say.

Sharing the power

The Scottish Parliament works to ensure that power is shared between the Scottish Government, the Parliament and the people of Scotland by:

- allocating time in the debating chamber for opposition MSPs to speak

- allowing any MSP, committee, private company or individual to propose a bill

- opening committee meetings to the public and listening to evidence from members of the public.

Accountability

The Scottish Parliament ensures that it holds the government to account and the people of Scotland hold the Parliament to account by:

- holding regular elections every four years which allow the Scottish people to get rid of MSPs who are not performing well
- having a voting system that makes sure everyone's vote counts
- ensuring all MSPs follow a strict code of conduct
- allowing MSPs to question government policies and actions in front of the public and on TV during First Minister's and Ministers' Questions.

What happens in the debating chamber?

On Wednesday afternoon and all day Thursday MSPs work in the debating chamber. During these times MSPs:

- speak on behalf of their **constituents**
- vote on **bills**
- question Government Ministers
- put forward motions (ideas) to be debated.

> **Constituent** a person living within a constituency represented by an MP or MSP.

> **Bill** a proposal for a law. A bill will only become a law after it has passed through Parliament and been signed by the Queen.

What happens in committees?

All day Tuesday and on Wednesday mornings MSPs work in committees. In these committees MSPs:

- examine new bills in detail
- call witnesses to give evidence
- conduct enquiries
- ask outside groups to give evidence
- discuss and write reports for the Parliament.

What happens in constituencies?

> **Constituency** The area an MP or MSP represents.

On Mondays and Fridays MSPs are at home in their **constituencies**. When they are working in their constituencies MSPs:

- meet with constituents
- answer letters, emails and telephone calls
- attend special events, such as opening a new library
- meet with local councillors and MPs
- work with their local political party.

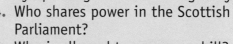
Show your understanding

1. What are the four founding principles of the Scottish Parliament?
2. How does the Scottish Parliament ensure it promotes equal opportunities?
3. Which of the four founding principles is met by allowing the public to attend meetings of the Scottish Parliament and by updating the website regularly?
4. Who shares power in the Scottish Parliament?
5. Who is allowed to propose a bill?
6. State two ways that the people of Scotland can hold the Parliament to account.
7. What happens on Mondays in the Scottish Parliament?
8. What happens on Wednesdays in the Scottish Parliament?

25 How are laws made?

By the end of this section you should be able to:
▶ Describe how laws are made in Westminster
▶ Describe how laws are made in Holyrood

In Westminster, bills need to pass through both the House of Commons and the House of Lords before they can be signed by the Queen and become law.

Westminster

First reading: An idea is introduced to the Parliament to explain to MPs the subject of the bill.

Second reading: The Government Minister in charge of the bill will explain what the bill is about and will answer questions. MPs then vote on the bill.

Committee stage: If the MPs vote 'yes' then the bill will be sent to a committee of about 5 to 15 MPs to **scrutinise** it.

Report stage: The committee will report back to the House of Commons and may suggest small changes called amendments.

Third reading: MPs then vote for a final time on the amended bill. If the majority vote 'yes' the bill then passes into the House of Lords.

In the House of Lords the bill goes through the same process as in the House of Commons, but at the committee stage all members of the House of Lords take part. This means that it can take a long time for a bill to pass through the House of Lords.

Scrutinise to examine in detail.

'Abstain'. (Abstain means that they do not wish to vote.)

In Westminster, MPs may not even be in the House of Commons when a vote is called. A bell will ring signalling eight minutes until a vote. MPs have to come from all over the Palace of Westminster to get to the 'Aye Lobby' or the 'No Lobby'. To vote, MPs have to walk through the appropriate lobby, the yes or the no.

Finally the bill passes to the Queen to be signed. This is called Royal Assent. The bill is now the law of the land.

Holyrood

Stage 1: A committee will examine the general ideas in the bill and will report to the Parliament. The committee will recommend whether or not the bill should be taken any further. The whole parliament will debate the main ideas of the bill, then vote.

If the majority vote 'yes', the bill will progress to Stage 2.

Stage 2: A committee will examine the bill in detail and may make amendments.

Stage 3: The whole Parliament will debate the bill and any amendments and then vote on the bill.

If the outcome is 'yes', the bill will progress to Royal Assent.

Royal Assent: The bill will be sent to the Queen to sign.

One major difference between Holyrood and Westminster is the way in which they vote on a bill. In Holyrood, they have a digital panel on the desk in front of them and they simply have to press 'Yes', 'No' or

 Show your understanding

1. What is the main difference between how laws are made in Westminster and in Holyrood?
2. What happens in the House of Commons?
3. Why can bills take a long time in the House of Lords?
4. What is Royal Assent?
5. Draw a flow diagram to show how bills are passed in the Scottish Parliament.

 Collect a skill

Identifying exaggeration
Remember that identifying exaggeration is an important skill in Modern Studies. If a person is exaggerating, they are making what they say sound better, more important or more significant than the evidence suggests.

> *The House of Lords has no power.*

This is the view of political student Amy Robertson. Could Amy Robertson be accused of exaggeration? Give reasons to support your answer.

? Bore your friends ...

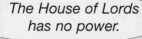

In Minnesota it is illegal to cross state lines with a duck on your head.

26 What are my rights? (1)

By the end of this chapter you should be able to:

► Explain why rights increase with age
► Give examples of rights you have
► Understand that along with every right, you have certain responsibilities

Rights

We hear a lot in the news about human rights, the rights of the child and the rights of the individual. But what does it all mean?

A right is something that a person can claim by law; something to which each person is entitled. Laws exist to protect your rights.

From birth you can:
Get your own passport
Have a bank or building society account

At age five you can:
See a U (Universal) certificate or PG (Parental Guidance) certificate film

At age twelve you can:
See a 12 certificate film
Buy a pet animal
State your views on your own adoption

At age fourteen you can:
Ride a horse on a road
Be employed part-time

At age sixteen you can:
Record a change of name officially
Leave school
Work full-time if you leave school
Get married
Have sex (with someone who is sixteen or over)
Drink wine or beer with a meal

At age seventeen you can:
Drive most vehicles
Donate blood
See your birth records if you are adopted

At age eighteen you can:
Vote
Get a tattoo
Buy alcohol
Work behind a bar
Buy fireworks

At age 21 you can:
Drive any vehicle
Be a candidate in European, parliamentary or local elections

Think about it! Why do you think that a person's rights increase as they get older?

What about responsibility?

With every right comes responsibility: things that are expected of you if you wish to keep your rights. For example, at age twelve you have the right to buy a pet but this means you also have the responsibility to take care of that pet. You must keep it clean and tidy up after it, feed it and exercise it. If you do not, you may lose the right to own the pet – your parents or even the RSPCA could take the pet from you. Similarly, at age seventeen you have the right to drive most motor vehicles but first you have the responsibility to sit and pass your driving test. Then you have the responsibility to drive according to the Highway Code, to insure, tax and MOT your vehicle and to drive safely.

Rights increase as you get older because the British legal system is based on the idea that people become more responsible as they grow older.

 Collect a skill

Class discussion!

Participating actively in a class discussion is not only an important skill to learn for Modern Studies but also a key skill for life! Read the two questions below and make notes about your thoughts on each question that will help you participate in a class discussion.

* Which right in the storyboard do you think is the one that comes with the biggest responsibility?
* Which right in the storyboard do you think can have the biggest consequences?

Remember the most important rule for successful class discussion is to listen! Never interrupt and always think carefully about what your classmates are saying before responding.

 Show your understanding

1. What is a right?
2. Write down three rights that you are entitled to now.
3. Choose three rights other than buying a pet and driving a car, and write down the responsibilities associated with them.
4. Are there any rights in Britain that you think are given at the wrong age? Give reasons for your answer.

REVIEW

Design a leaflet, poster or webpage for young people which tells them about their rights.

27 What are my rights? (2)

What are we exploring?

By the end of this section you should be able to:

▶ Explain why some rights are fundamental

▶ Understand why special protection is needed for children's rights

📁 Collect a skill

Boost your word power!
Don't forget to use the glossary boxes to help you learn new words and boost your word power.

The European **Convention** on Human Rights sets out the basic human rights thought to be important in a **civilised** society. In Britain a law was passed in 1998 to protect these rights. It came into force in 2000 and is known as the Human Rights Act.

> **Convention** a formal agreement between country leaders, politicians and states on a matter which involves them all.

> **Civilised** this describes a society or country that has a highly developed system of government, culture and way of life and that treats its people fairly.

These rights are often referred to as fundamental human rights. This means that they are the most important human rights. They include:

- The right to life; **prohibition** of torture; prohibition of slavery; abolition of the death penalty.
- The right to **liberty** and security, and to a fair trial.
- The right to respect for private and family life; the right to marry; the protection of property; the right to education.
- Freedom of thought and religion; freedom of expression; freedom of assembly; the right to free elections.

> **Prohibition** when something is forbidden.

> **Liberty** freedom.

⚙️ Activate your brain cells!

Think about it! Read each of the fundamental human rights again carefully. Think of a reason why each one is important and discuss these with a partner. Are there any of the rights you do not understand?

The language may seem confusing and some of it may not apply to you at the moment, which is why there are separate rights set out in international law to protect children. In 1989, world leaders decided that children under eighteen needed special protection. The UN Convention on the Rights of the Child is a legally binding agreement between 192 of the world's countries.

There are 54 articles in the Convention and each article sets out a specific right. Some of these have been included in the source.

The Convention is extremely important because it gives all countries and organisations a reference point for basic rights. Almost all the countries in the world have agreed to the Convention. It has been successful in encouraging countries to include children in their human rights laws and to listen to children. Unfortunately, despite so many countries agreeing to the Convention, there are still countries in the world where children's rights are not well protected and where many of the rights in the Convention are not met.

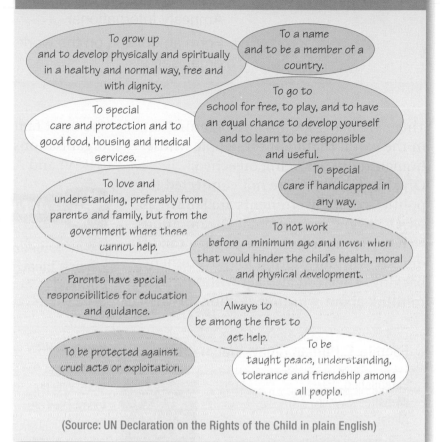

All children are protected by the Convention no matter their race, colour, sex, language, religion, political or other opinion, or where they were born or who they were born to.

Every child has the right:

To grow up and to develop physically and spiritually in a healthy and normal way, free and with dignity.

To a name and to be a member of a country.

To special care and protection and to good food, housing and medical services.

To go to school for free, to play, and to have an equal chance to develop yourself and to learn to be responsible and useful.

To love and understanding, preferably from parents and family, but from the government where these cannot help.

To special care if handicapped in any way.

To not work before a minimum age and never when that would hinder the child's health, moral and physical development.

Parents have special responsibilities for education and guidance.

Always to be among the first to get help.

To be taught peace, understanding, tolerance and friendship among all people.

To be protected against cruel acts or exploitation.

(Source: UN Declaration on the Rights of the Child in plain English)

Stretch yourself

Imagine you are an **ambassador** for the UN. Write a letter to the leader of a country that does not have a good record on human rights. In this letter you should explain why protecting human rights is important.

Ambassador an important official who represents a country or an organisation.

REVIEW

Design a poster, leaflet or webpage about the rights protected by the UN Convention on the Rights of the Child.

 Show your understanding

1. What has Britain done to ensure that basic human rights are protected?
2. Choose two of the fundamental rights guaranteed by the Human Rights Act and explain why they are important.
3. Which of the fundamental human rights do you think is the most important? Give reasons for your answer.
4. Why do you think that there is a separate agreement for the rights of the child?
5. Choose three of the rights of the child and explain why you think they are important.
6. Has the Convention on the Rights of the Child made a difference?

Does anyone fight for human rights?

By the end of this section you should be able to:

▶ Discuss the work of Human Rights Watch (HRW) and Amnesty International

▶ Form an opinion on the work of international organisations

There are many groups and organisations in the world that fight for people whose human rights are being breached. Organisations that are not connected to politicians or governments are known as NGOs: Non-Governmental Organisations. NGOs are important because they can act quickly without waiting for government backing. They can also act without having to think about winning elections. Two of the most famous and most successful organisations are Human Rights Watch (HRW) and Amnesty International.

 Activate your brain cells!

Why do people whose human rights are being breached need help? Discuss your thoughts in a small group.

Factfile 1: Human Rights Watch (HRW)

Established: 1978
Website: www.hrw.org
Aims:

Logo:

HUMAN RIGHTS WATCH

- To prevent discrimination.
- To bring those who breach human rights to justice.
- To investigate and expose human rights abuses.
- To challenge governments to end abusive practices and respect international human rights law.
- To recruit people to support the cause of human rights for all.

What does HRW do?

HRW investigates human rights abuses and reports on them all over the world. They use the world's television channels and newspapers to draw attention to places in the world where human rights are being abused. They meet with governments, the United Nations, the European Union and the African Union, along with other organisations, to try and bring human rights abusers to justice. HRW uses the media to persuade governments to listen.

Where is HRW working just now?

Child labour is a major problem in some areas of the world with hundreds of millions of children working today. They are being denied an education and are often forced to work in unhealthy and dangerous conditions. HRW reported in February 2009 on children working in Indonesia.

Hundreds of thousands of girls in Indonesia are employed as domestic servants in other people's households. Some of these girls are as young as eleven. They are cooking, cleaning, doing laundry, and looking after other people's children. Most of the girls are working more than twelve hours a day, seven days a week. Almost all of the girls earn a tiny amount of money and some earn none at all. Some of the girls in the HRW report were being abused physically, psychologically and sexually.

Factfile 2: Amnesty International

Established: 1961
Website: www.amnesty.org

Logo:

Aims:
To conduct research and generate action to prevent and end grave abuses of human rights and to demand justice for those whose rights have been violated.

What does Amnesty International do?
Amnesty International campaigns all over the world to ensure that every person has basic human rights. They research human rights abuses and take actions to end these abuses. They put pressure on governments to protect rights and bring justice to those who are suffering. Examples of the actions they take include: stopping violence against women; defending the rights and dignity of those trapped in poverty; fighting to abolish the death penalty; and protecting the rights of refugees and migrants.

Amnesty International uses its massive membership of more than 2.2 million to persuade governments to listen.

Where is Amnesty International working just now?
Hundreds of thousands of children around the world are experiencing the brutality of war as child soldiers. Children are often abducted from their homes or schools and recruited into military groups. Some enlist voluntarily because their lives are so affected by war that they do not see any other option.

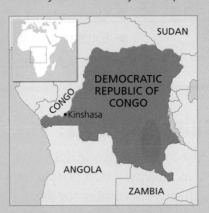

Amnesty reported on the situation in the Democratic Republic of Congo (DRC) in April 2009. Child soldiers who try to escape are killed or tortured, sometimes in front of other children, to discourage further escapes. Children as young as seven years old are drugged, given guns and ammunition and sent out to fight. Amnesty International is working with the government to free child soldiers and help them reintegrate into society.

Show your understanding

1. What is an NGO?
2. What similarities can you spot in the aims of the two organisations?
3. What is the problem in Indonesia?
4. What is the problem in the DRC?
5. Look carefully at the logos for the two organisations. Think about what they do and what they stand for. Choose one of the organisations and design a new logo.

Stretch yourself
How do you feel about what is happening in the Democratic Republic of Congo?

REVIEW What is the main difference between Human Rights Watch and Amnesty International in the way they persuade governments to listen?

How are rights protected?

What are we exploring?

By the end of this chapter you should be able to:

▶ Understand why there are rules

▶ Explain the difference between rules and laws

▶ Use your imagination to write in detail

What are rules and laws?

Rules and laws exist to protect your rights. When people live in groups, when people live together, eat together, work or play together, there have to be rules which make sure that people treat each other fairly. If there were no rules then there would be chaos.

Imagine if there were no rules in school. Pupils would turn up when they liked, treat teachers and other pupils however they wanted, skip lessons and maybe skip school altogether. This might sound like fun for a day or two, but eventually everyone would get fed up. All children have the right to an education, and without rules in school it would be very difficult to protect this right.

Imagine if there were no rules on the football or hockey pitch. There would be no point in playing because there would never be a clear winner and people might get hurt.

 Activate your brain cells!

Think about it! Imagine life with no rules. Discuss with a partner what you would do if there were no rules for one day.

What are laws?

Laws are rules which have passed through Parliament and been signed by the Queen. Unlike rules which can change depending upon which school you are in or who your parents are, laws do not change. Once a law has been passed it applies to the whole country. The UK Parliament makes laws for the whole of the UK but Scotland has its own legal system. This means that some laws are different in Scotland from the rest of the UK.

One example of a law which is different in Scotland from the rest of the UK is the length of time a suspect can be held in custody without charge. In Scotland a suspect must be released after six hours but in England and Wales a suspect can be held for twenty-four hours.

There are many different kinds of laws. Some laws protect property, some protect you as an individual and some do both, such as the Highway Code. The Highway Code is the name given to the collection of laws and rules that apply to the road. The Highway Code applies to Scotland, England and Wales.

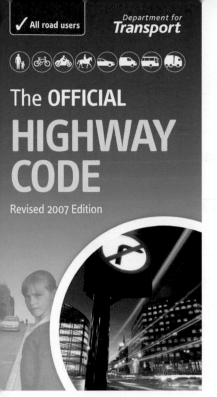

✓ All road users

Department for
Transport

The **OFFICIAL**

HIGHWAY CODE

Revised 2007 Edition

Laws are made by the people we elect to represent us in Parliament. Rules can be made by anyone. In school, rules are usually made by the head teacher. At home, rules are made by your parents. On the football pitch, rules are made by FIFA and in Disneyland the rules are made by the manager of the park.

There are many different people and groups who protect you. Starting closest to home, your parents/guardians are your primary carers. This is why your parents will have their own rules. Every parent will have different ideas about what is best for their children and about how best to protect them and so will have different rules. Teachers also have the job of protecting you and looking after your rights. While you are at school your teachers are responsible for your care and so they make sure you and others follow the school rules.

In the wider community there are other groups of people who protect you and look after your rights: the police, fire fighters, the coastguard and paramedics. Together they are known as the emergency services.

Learning link

How are laws made?

So if rules and laws are there to protect us, who **enforces** the laws?
Who protects you?

> Enforce make sure that people obey.

 Collect a skill

Imagine!

Using your imagination is an important skill to develop for life. It helps you think your way out of your environment and call on your previous knowledge. Close your eyes and create a movie board in your head.

Use your imagination to write a short story about the day when there were no rules.

 Show your understanding

1. Why do we need rules and laws?
2. What is the difference between rules and laws?
3. Who makes laws?
4. Write down ten examples of dangerous things that could happen if there was no Highway Code. Make sure that you think of all road users – cyclists, drivers, pedestrians, etc.
5. Make a list of all the people you can think of who protect your rights.

30 How do the police protect my rights?

What are we exploring?

By the end of this section you should be able to:

▶ Describe the duties of the police
▶ Explain how the powers of the police allow them to protect us

The Police Force is the main group of people who enforce laws and protect our rights from people who break the law.

Activate your brain cells!

Why do we need the police? In a small group talk about what life would be like without the police. Try to come up with lots of different scenarios.

Police officers have six main duties:

I protect and reassure the community.

I uphold the law.

I prevent crimes from taking place.

I control road traffic.

I keep the peace.

I detect and investigate criminals.

In order to carry out their duties and protect us the police need to have powers that other members of society do not have. There are five key powers that police officers have to help them do their jobs well.

Gather evidence

The police may gather evidence such as photos, fingerprints, saliva samples and footwear impressions. This allows them to match evidence taken from crime scenes to suspects.

Custody

The police can take a suspect into custody while they are investigating a crime. In Scotland they can do this for six hours and then they must arrest or release the suspect. In England and Wales a suspect can be held for twenty-four hours. If the suspect is suspected of terrorist activity, they can be held for up to seven days without being charged.

Stop and search

The police can stop anyone and ask where they are going and what they are doing but they can only search a person if they have a good reason. For example, they may search someone who they suspect is in possession of a gun or drugs.

Arrest

The police can arrest someone who has committed a crime or someone they suspect of having committed a crime. Usually the police will have to have a warrant to arrest a suspect but there are some circumstances where an arrest can be made on the spot. These include someone caught in the act of committing a crime, someone seen running away from the scene of a crime pursued by others, or someone threatening danger to the public.

Caution

Not all crimes have to go through the courts. For low-level crimes the police will issue a caution. This is not a criminal conviction but will be recorded on the police database.

What is it like being a police officer?

Name: Amy MacDonald

Age: 24

Qualifications: BA Applied Social Sciences, Highers in English, Modern Studies, Physical Education and Computing.

What is your job title? Police Constable

What is your favourite part of the job? There are many things that I get to do in my job that give me a sense of fulfilment. One of my favourite duties is carrying out enquiries into the activities of those involved in the supply of controlled drugs. I like the opportunity to combat the supply of drugs. I think it is often easy to forget that Police Officers are ordinary people doing an extraordinary job. I get to work with some amazing people.

What is the worst part of your job? The best bits of my job far outweigh any bad. Seeing a young life ruined by drugs or a family affected by the loss of a young relative as a result of a road traffic collision are probably the worst parts of my job.

Collect a skill

Memory mapping!

Learning how to draw memory maps will help you in your school subjects. Memory mapping is a method you can use to help you organise your thoughts. In the middle of your page draw a circle and write 'powers of the police' inside it. Now draw five lines coming out from the circle. It should look like the diagram below. Use the text to help you write a small amount about each of the powers and add in some pictures.

POWERS OF THE POLICE

Show your understanding

1. What are the duties of a police officer?
2. Which of the powers of the police do you think is most important? Give reasons for your answer.
3. Read the interview with PC Amy MacDonald carefully. What is her favourite part of the job?
4. Imagine that you are a police officer and you are being interviewed like PC Amy MacDonald. What do you think would be your favourite part of the job? What would be the worst part?

? Bore your friends...

The song 'Message in a Bottle' by The Police was at number one in the UK chart for three weeks in September 1979.

31 What do paramedics do?

What are we exploring?

By the end of this section you should be able to:

▶ Describe the work of a paramedic
▶ Describe how the Scottish Ambulance Service responds to major incidents
▶ Discuss the difficulties involved in a paramedic's role

The Scottish Ambulance Service has two main roles – the emergency service and the patient transport service.

The people who drive ambulances and attend to patients in emergencies are called paramedics. They have a very difficult job as they have to get to the scene of an accident quickly and then treat people at the scene. Often people require immediate treatment and paramedics have to do this without all of the equipment that doctors have in hospitals. Sometimes paramedics have to treat patients in very difficult circumstances, such as someone trapped in very stormy weather or at the scene of a large road traffic accident.

Paramedics usually work with an ambulance technician to help them. However, they might work on their own, using a motorbike, emergency response car or even a bicycle to reach their patients. With extra training, they could also become members of an air ambulance crew.

 Activate your brain cells!

Think about what it would be like to be a paramedic. Close your eyes and imagine yourself arriving first at the scene of an accident. How do you think you would react? How do you think you would feel? What would you see? What would you do first?

The Scottish Ambulance Service has an air ambulance section which has two helicopters and two fixed-wing aeroplanes. The Air Wing can be extremely important for patients who live in rural areas far from their nearest hospital, especially in the islands. The helicopters are based in Inverness and Glasgow. The planes are based in Glasgow and Aberdeen.

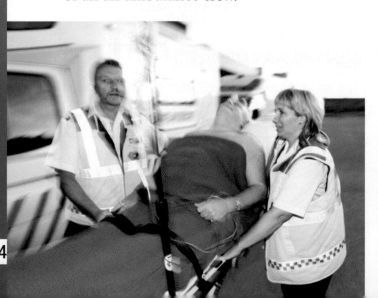

Identifying exaggeration!

> The Scottish Ambulance Service cannot deal with emergency situations in remote rural areas.

What evidence is there in the text that this statement is exaggerated?

What happens when someone dials 999?

The Scottish Ambulance Service's key role is to respond to 999 calls as quickly as possible. On average ambulance crews in Scotland respond to around half a million emergency calls every year. When a 999 call comes in, the people on the end of the phone use very modern computer software to help them to categorise the call into classifications A, B or C. A category A call is life-threatening. This is the most serious type of call and it is given priority over all others. A category B call is serious but not life-threatening. Category C calls are neither life-threatening nor serious. Often the caller may not need emergency assistance and may be referred to their GP or other NHS agency.

How do paramedics deal with major incidents?

Sometimes paramedics have to respond to major incidents. Examples in Scotland include the terrorist attacks at Glasgow airport, the shootings at Dunblane Primary School and the explosion at the Stockline Plastics factory in Glasgow.

When a large-scale incident occurs all of the emergency services have to work closely together. The Scottish Ambulance Service has identified four priorities when in a major incident situation:

- Responding to the scene quickly and setting up a system to prioritise and treat patients based on their medical needs.
- Treating and caring for anyone who may be injured.
- Stabilising and transporting patients who need further treatment to hospital.
- Supporting and treating any other emergency responders who may receive injuries in the course of their operations at the scene.

Show your understanding

1. What number would you dial in an emergency?
2. Why might a helicopter be needed?
3. What makes a paramedic's job difficult?
4. How many people normally work in an ambulance?
5. 'An ambulance will be sent out for every 999 call.' Is this statement true or false? Provide reasons to support your answer.
6. What are two of the priorities of the Scottish Ambulance Service when dealing with a major incident?

REVIEW

Make some notes to help you discuss the following question as a class:

What problems might a paramedic face when dealing with an emergency situation?

> ### What are we exploring?
>
> **By the end of this section you should be able to:**
> ▶ Explain why an organised fire service is important
> ▶ Describe the work of the fire service

Firefighters are part of the emergency services. They play an important role in protecting people in the community.

How did the Fire Service begin?

Ever since man discovered fire he has also been fighting to control the flames. During the Middle Ages, many towns and cities simply burned down because there were no organised fire-fighting arrangements and because most homes were built of wood.

After the Great Fire of London in 1666, things began to change. People demanded a more organised fire service. The problem was that buildings were only protected if they bought an insurance policy. Buildings that owned a policy were given a badge, or fire mark, to fix to their building. If a fire started, the fire service was called. They looked for the fire mark and, provided it was the right one, the fire would be dealt with. Often the buildings were left to burn until the right company attended! The authorities in Edinburgh formed the city's

first properly organised brigade in 1824. Today there are 63 brigades in England, Wales, Scotland and Northern Ireland.

Collect a skill

Identifying bias!

> If the Great Fire of London hadn't happened, the UK would still not have a modern organised fire service.

This is the view of a London historian. Why could the London historian be accused of being biased?

What do firefighters do?

Firefighters are usually seen in movies and on TV fighting fires and rescuing people from burning buildings. However, firefighters use lots of different skills to respond to a range of incidents. They can be called to deal with hazardous materials,

to road traffic accidents, to help people who are trapped, and even to water rescues.

The fire service is also involved in non-emergency work. They carry out safety checks in the home and advise on fire safety at work, as well as fire safety inspections for businesses. They also offer a range of training courses so that people can learn about fire safety.

Being a firefighter requires a special kind of person who can not only face danger and remain calm but who can also look after the public and comfort people when they are in distress.

One important job for a firefighter is to teach children about the dangers of fire. The Central Scotland Fire Service has nine rules that they use to get the message across:

1. Never play with matches or lighters.
2. Never play with a lighted candle.
3. Don't play close to a fire or heater, or leave toys near a fire or heater.
4. Don't pull on electric cables or fiddle with electrical appliances or sockets.
5. Never switch on the cooker.
6. Never put anything on top of the cooker.
7. Don't touch any saucepans on the cooker.
8. Don't put things on top of heaters or lights.
9. If you see matches or lighters lying around, tell a grown-up.

What problems do firefighters face?

Every year hundreds of silly and careless acts cost firefighters critical minutes which could be used to save people who are in real danger. At least half a million pounds was wasted in 2008 on hoax calls and deliberate fires in Scotland. Hundreds of

hours of firefighters' time are wasted and lives are put at risk. Firefighters are forced to spend time dealing with false alarms and preventable blazes while people are trapped elsewhere.

Scottish Sheriffs take hoax calls very seriously. Between September 2008 and December 2009 four men were sent to jail for hoax calls to the fire service. In June 2008, in Sheffield, a fire engine that was responding to a hoax call crashed killing a woman and seriously injuring her daughter.

 Show your understanding

1. What was the problem with the way that fires were dealt with in London after the Great Fire of London?
2. Apart from fires, what other kinds of duties do firefighters carry out?
3. Give an example of non-emergency fire service work.
4. Why do you think that the fire service sees teaching children about fire as important?
5. Are hoax calls dangerous?

Stretch yourself

Imagine that you have just been appointed as the Chief Safety Officer of your local fire brigade. You need to come up with a new plan for teaching primary school children about the dangers of fire. (Make sure you include the nine rules.) What techniques would you use? Create a piece of work to show off your ideas, such as a leaflet or a storyboard for a cartoon.

? Bore your friends ...

The Great Fire of London started in a bakery in Pudding Lane because Thomas Farriner's maid forgot to put the ovens out at the end of the night. Thomas Farriner was the King's baker!

33 Who protects our rights at sea?

What are we exploring?

By the end of this section you should be able to:
▶ Describe the work of the coastguard
▶ Describe the work of the RNLI

We need people to protect our rights at sea as well as on land. The Maritime and Coastguard Agency (MCA) aims to prevent the loss of lives on the coast and at sea. They make sure that ships are safe and they work to prevent coastal pollution. Their motto is 'Safer Lives, Safer Ships, Cleaner Seas'.

Maritime and Coastguard Agency

The MCA is in charge of safety at sea. The agency co-ordinates all rescues and decides what kind of rescue is needed. Sometimes this will be a helicopter, sometimes a cliff rescue team and sometimes a lifeboat. If a lifeboat is required, the Royal National Lifeboat Institution (RNLI) is needed.

Lifeboats

The RNLI was founded in 1824. Since 1824 it has saved more than 139,000 lives at sea. In 2009 it rescued an average of 22 people per day. The RNLI is a voluntary organisation, which means that the crew members do not get paid for the work they do. They give up their time to carry out rescues in difficult and often dangerous conditions. The RNLI is a charity, which means it relies on fundraising and donations. It provides a 24-hour lifesaving service around the UK and Republic of Ireland.

What is it like being a crew member for the RNLi?

Jamie Anderson

How old were you when you started working as a crew member?

Nineteen

What do you wear on the lifeboat?

We wear a full-length woolly suit, called a woolly bear, under a drysuit. We also wear a lifejacket, a helmet with a visor, boots and gloves.

What is it like being a crew member?

Brilliant – I love it! It's great to be able to help people when they are in difficulty. It's very exciting when we get a call-out and the sea is rough, and it's great to be part of such a close team who are all committed to helping others.

How do you feel when you get called out in the middle of a cold winter night?

It's hard to get out of a warm bed when you've just been woken up but there's always a rush of adrenaline when the pager goes off that makes you get up.

What is it like on the lifeboat when the weather is really bad?

It can be scary at times but we are all well trained and the boats are more than capable of handling the conditions.

What was your most dramatic shout?

Rescuing a deaf fisherman who was cut off by the incoming tide on rocks. It was dark, communication was difficult and it was very cold.

How dangerous is your job as a crew member?

Being a crew member can be dangerous because of the weather conditions we often find ourselves in, but we are very well trained by the RNLI, which considerably reduces the risks.

What made you want to join the lifeboat crew?

My family have always been volunteers for the RNLI. I like the social side of being part of the lifeboat crew, too, and the feeling of being a part of a team.

How do you keep fit?

I watch what I eat, and general day-to-day duties and my hobbies keep me fit.

What is the worst part of being lifeboat crew?

Sometimes it can be boring but the lives we save always make up for it.

Do you ever get frightened when you are about to go out on a rescue?

Yes – if the sea is rough it can be frightening but also exciting.

Show your understanding

1. What is the MCA?
2. What different types of rescues do the MCA co-ordinate?
3. Do the crew members for the RNLI get paid for the work that they do?
4. What made Jamie join the RNLI?
5. What is the most dramatic rescue that Jamie has done?
6. Why does Jamie like being an RNLI crew member?
7. Would you like to be an RNLI crew member? Give reasons for your answer.
8. What do you think about the MCA logo? Imagine the MCA has decided their logo is old-fashioned and out-of-date. You have just been hired to design a new logo for the MCA. Use the information in the text and their motto to help you with ideas.

REVIEW

What is the difference between the RNLI and the MCA? What would our lives be like at sea if people did not volunteer for the RNLI? Can you think of ways to encourage people to volunteer for the RNLI?

34 Why should we study China?

By the end of this section you should be able to:

▶ Explain why China is an interesting country to study

▶ Explain what communism is

How does China's history affect its present?

China is one of the oldest countries in the world. It has a long history of working together and obedience to the state. In 1949 Mao Zedong set up the People's Republic of China. At that time most of China's people were peasants and workers. They had been ruled by the wealthy bourgeoisie (middle-class people) for a long time and were fed up being poor and hungry. They tried to force the bourgeoisie

Mao Zedong (Chairman Mao)

China factfile

China is the fourth largest country in the world.

China shares borders with fourteen different countries.

One fifth of the world's population lives in China: 1.3 billion people.

China has one of the fastest growing economies in the world.

China has the largest workforce in the world.

China has massive military power.

China has one of five permanent seats on the UN Security Council.

to share the money and property but the bourgeoisie fought back. However, the peasants and workers were too powerful and eventually took control of China. Their new leader, Mao Zedong, promised that now everyone would be equal: poverty would no longer be a problem.

Mao believed that communism was the best economic system in the world. He thought that communism would make China's people better off and more powerful. Communism is an ideology – a set of beliefs or ideas.

Is this how our economic system works?

The opposite of communism is capitalism. This is the economic system that we have in Britain. This means that people in Britain are allowed to own goods and property. If people work hard, they can be successful and rich individuals. Other capitalist countries include France, Canada and the USA.

What is communism?

The Chinese political system is based upon the ideas of a nineteenth-century philosopher called Karl Marx. He believed that all countries passed through all phases in history – first feudalism, second capitalism and third communism. (Feudalism was the old medieval system of landlords and peasants.) Marx predicted that the most industrial countries (UK and Germany) would become communist first, but in 1917 Russia, led by Vladimir Lenin, was the first country to experience a communist revolution. When Chairman

Mao led China towards communism in 1949 he was following this belief.

Mao believed that support for communism would begin in the countryside and so he built up support there first. Communism is based on the idea that everyone is equal. The state controls all resources, land and property, and allows the people equal access. Mao's political party is called the Communist Party of China (CPC).

Today China is still a communist country but it has opened up its economy to the rest of the world and many aspects of life are very different from the way they were under the old form of Chinese communism. The people of China today have a lot more freedom than they used to have and people can now change their lifestyles by making a success of their own business.

Show your understanding

1. How many countries does China share its border with?
2. How many people live in China?
3. What is the main language in China?
4. What did Mao Zedong promise when he took over China?
5. What is communism?
6. Is Scotland a communist country?

❓ Bore your friends…

The Great Wall of China is not visible from space. The only man-made structures you can see from space are the Pyramids of Giza and the Hoover Dam.

REVIEW Design a mini tourist brochure about China. Include the basic facts you have learnt here and use the Internet to find out more about China's history, its people, its geography and its traditions.

35 What is life like for workers in China?

By the end of this section you should be able to:

▶ Explain what an economy is

▶ Provide examples of people who have not benefited from China's economic boom

When Chairman Mao died in 1976 there was a fight for control of China. Four of Mao's closest friends (the Gang of Four) tried to take power after his death but were arrested and convicted of crimes against the state. Eventually Deng Xiaoping took control of the Communist Party of China (CPC).

Since Deng came to power in 1978 China has changed a lot. It has opened its doors to trade with the rest of the world and many foreign companies now invest in China. This has meant that China's **economy** has boomed and it is now one of the fastest-growing economies in the world. However, not everyone has benefited from China's economic boom and some people have been left behind.

> **Economy** the way a country makes and uses money.

Who are the Mingong?

China's booming economic growth in the major cities has created a demand for cheap migrant labour from the countryside. These migrant workers (people who move to find work) are known as the Mingong. The flow of people into the cities has been described as the biggest movement of human population since the world began. The 'floating population' of China is estimated to be at least 100 million people.

Activate your brain cells!

Think about it! Close your eyes and try to imagine what life would be like to be one of the Mingong.

What do the Mingong do?

The Mingong provide the cheap labour that allows China to produce many of the items that it sells to the rest of the world. The country is sometimes called 'the workshop of the world'. China makes 66 per cent of the world's microwave ovens, 50 per cent of our clothes, 50 per cent of the world's cameras, 30 per cent of our computers and 25 per cent of our washing machines.

Collect a skill

Presenting statistics!

If you are carrying out research in Modern Studies, you may need to present statistics in a way that is easy to read. Often a simple bar graph is the best way to show statistics. Remember that a bar graph should have a title, clear labels and a scale. Look at the statistics that describe China as the 'workshop of the world'. Draw a bar graph to show the statistics.

In China, those connected to the CPC get rich, while the Mingong work for little money, often in the most dangerous conditions. They are hidden from view and kept away from the world's TV cameras and reporters. Some agricultural workers are paid only 60 pence an hour. At the same time, China's rich can afford to pay the annual fee to play at the world's largest golf club – Mission Hills, in Hong Kong. Memberships cost between 428,000 yuan to 1.68 million yuan (£42,000 to £167,000).

What does this mean for the people?

A Bang Bang man hard at work

Chongqing is the fastest-growing city in the world, with 31 million people living in its greater area and 1 million more arriving every year. The average annual income is around £3,000. A migrant worker will be lucky to earn one fifth of this. However, in the countryside there is mass unemployment and those who do work earn tiny amounts of money. In China the gap between the rich and the poor is growing and is one of the largest in the world.

What is the Bang Bang Army?

The city of Chongqing is built on steep hills in Western China. Any visitor arriving in Chongqing is immediately struck by the large numbers of men carrying heavy loads on their bamboo poles (bang bang). This group of 100,000 hard-working men is known locally as the Bang Bang Army.

Made up of peasant farmers flocking to the city in their thousands, the men are willing to do anything to make a living. Many of them have left their families at home because they cannot afford to feed them or send them to school. The Bang Bang Army work long days and carry heavy loads around the streets of Chongqing for very little money. An average day's work would pay approximately 20 yuan (£1.90).

Stretch yourself

Why do you think there are no Bang Bang men in Britain? What makes China different?

Show your understanding

1. What is an economy?
2. Why is China's economy important?
3. Have the Mingong benefited from China's economic boom? Provide evidence to support your view.
4. Imagine what life is like in Chongqing, the fastest-growing city in the world. Write three words in your jotter to describe the sounds, smells and look of the expanding city.

? Bore your friends ...

China has more English speakers than the USA.

Is everyone in China really equal?

What are we exploring?

By the end of this section you should be able to:
▶ Discuss inequalities and give examples from China

Communism is based on the idea that everyone is equal. The original communists who took part in the 1949 revolution in China fought because they believed that all people should be treated the same and that the government should control resources for everyone's benefit. Many of them were peasants fighting against the rich landowners for an equal standard of living. So, is everyone in China really equal?

 Activate your brain cells!

How can we tell if everyone in a country is equal? Discuss this with a partner.

What is the Hukou?

Migrant workers (Mingong) in China face the problem of the Hukou permit system. The Hukou was introduced in 1955. People were classified as urban or rural. In order to receive many state benefits, such as education or certain types of work permits,

you had to be officially registered in your town or rural county. This made it very hard to legally move around the country.

In the 1900s the Chinese government began stopping the Hukou, and by 2009 eleven out of twenty-three provinces had abolished it. The process is slow because many people rely on it for their benefits in old age.

Housing inequalities

The combination of the economic boom in China since 1978 and a shortage of space has meant that house prices and rents in cities are rising fast. Rapid urban growth has placed massive pressure on transport, housing, energy supplies, and water and sanitation in the cities. The supply of housing is struggling to meet the demand, although it is generally considered that housing conditions have improved for most people.

While China was under communist control, party membership and status were important factors in the allocation of housing. Since 1999, all existing properties have been sold to tenants, and private developers have been encouraged to build new housing projects.

What is life like in the countryside?

More than half of China's population lives in the countryside – 57 per cent. The Chinese government admits that more than half of the rural population have no money for a doctor, even if they could find one locally. In some villages no one has a bike, far less a car. There is often no running water, toilets or electricity. What money there is comes from the migrants returning home with their savings.

Are there inequalities in education?

Children in China are required to undergo nine years of compulsory education. In most areas this is achieved but there are regions where many children drop out before completing nine years. This is largely due to the fact that although education is compulsory, it is not free.

Standards of education also vary enormously across the country. In Tibet only half of the population can read and write and less than 1.5 per cent receives secondary education. On the other hand, in cities like Beijing and Shanghai about 60 per cent of children receive secondary education and nearly 98 per cent of people can read and write.

Collect a skill

Support with evidence!

> Some parts of China have poorer education than others.

Do you agree with this statement? Provide evidence to support your view.

What about communism?

China's leaders still see themselves, and the country, as communist. The communists justify the inequality and the poverty with the idea that the country needs to develop industrially in order to become fully communist. They see individual sacrifices as being for the greater good.

 Show your understanding

1. How did the Hukou prevent people from making choices about their lives?
2. What evidence is there that the massive movement of people into China's cities is having a negative effect on housing standards?
3. Do you think people will have fairer access to housing now that the Communist Party has less control? Why or why not?
4. How do the leaders of China view the inequalities that exist in China? Is this fair?
5. Do you think that communism has worked in China?

❓ Bore your friends...

Hong Kong is the city with the most Rolls Royce cars per person in the world.

37 What is life like in rural China?

Rural China is home to the poorest of China's population. Life in the countryside has not modernised in the same way as it has in the urban areas.

> **Rural** the countryside.

 Activate your brain cells!

Think about it! Can you think of any reasons why China's countryside is home to the poorest people in China?

What was life in the countryside like?

After the communist revolution in 1949, the Chinese government took control of **agriculture** and by 1958 the People's Communes had been formed. These were large farming units where the peasants lived and worked together. People were made to work for the communes and had very little control over their lives. Even private cooking was banned; everyone had to cook and eat together. Everything previously owned by families – animals, stored grains and other food items – had to be given to the commune. Family life was eliminated. Nurseries for babies and homes for the elderly were set up. Everybody in the commune was given a job by their commune leaders.

> **Agriculture** cultivating land, growing crops, breeding, feeding and raising animals; farming.

By the 1960s, Chinese farming was in serious trouble and people were starving. The communes were not producing enough food and prices were too high, so that many people could not afford food. Estimates suggest that between 1959 and 1962 more than 20 million people died of starvation.

When Deng came to power in 1978 he began to modernise the Chinese economy and farming system. He scrapped the People's Communes and replaced them with a system called household responsibility. The new system meant that farmers were each given small plots of land for their family. They were allowed to decide what to grow and could sell it at private markets for the best price they could get.

This was good for some families, who were able to grow good crops and successfully sell them at market. Some farmers became wealthy and were able to buy their neighbours' land, which gave them bigger farms and more profit. Other families were not so lucky and had to work hard to make the most from their small plots.

What is it like in the countryside today?

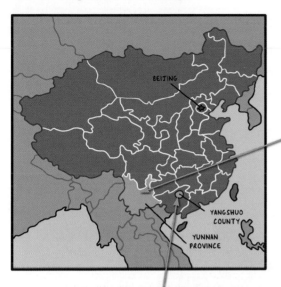

Case Study 2: Rice paddies in Yunnan Province

Farming in China has always been labour-intensive. This means that people have to work very hard on a small area of land.

China has a large population and it is difficult to find enough land to cultivate. Rice is China's most important crop and accounts for 25 per cent of China's cultivated land. Rice is grown in paddies: flooded fields which are also home to fish that are eaten by the farmers. Every scrap of land is used because the farmers depend upon the crops to feed their families.

Everyone in the family helps in the paddies. It is back-breaking work and there is no modern technology to help make life easier. The only help for the farmers is the oxen used to plough the fields.

Case study 1: Cormorant fishing in Yangshuo County

In the area around Yangshuo County in Guangxi Province in southern China people still fish using old-fashioned methods. Fishermen do not use nets or lines but cormorants. Cormorants are birds which can dive deep under water and hold their breath for a long time while they look for fish. The fishermen loosely tie string around the cormorant's neck to prevent it from swallowing the large fish. When the birds come to the surface they deposit the fish on the fisherman's bamboo raft.

Show your understanding

1. Where do the poorest people in China live?
2. What were the People's Communes?
3. What was the problem with the People's Communes?
4. How did Deng modernise China's farming?

   Deng's modernisations were successful for all.

5. Do you agree with this statement? Give reasons for your answer.
6. What is cormorant fishing?
7. What does the phrase labour-intensive mean?
8. Do you think that life in rural China is hard? Explain your answer.

38 What is happening in Tibet?

Before examining the issue of Tibet it is important to learn a bit about China's record on human rights. China's communist culture focuses on society as a whole, not on the individual. In Scotland and Britain, where culture focuses on the individual, the government works to protect every individual and to make society the best it can be for all. In China, the government works to improve life for the group and so sometimes individuals are left behind.

 Activate your brain cells!

What do you think about a society where the individual is sacrificed for the good of all?

Human Rights Watch (HRW) and Amnesty International have been highlighting human rights abuses in China ever since the organisations began their work. In the run-up to the Beijing Olympic Games in 2008, China had to address many of these issues and make an effort to improve life for all of its citizens. However, the issue of Tibet, among others, continues to worry human rights groups.

Learning link

Does anyone fight for human rights?

How did the Tibetan issue begin?

Tibet is part of China that believes it was invaded in 1949 and wants to be independent. Free Tibet is a pressure group that works all across the world to raise awareness of the issues in Tibet. They claim that the Chinese occupation has resulted in the death of over one million Tibetans; the destruction of over 6,000 monasteries, nunneries and temples; and the imprisonment and torture of thousands of Tibetans.

The Dalai Lama, Tibet's political and spiritual leader, fled Tibet in 1959 to Dharamsala, in India, and was followed by over 100,000 Tibetans. Here he established the Tibetan Government in Exile. In 1989 he was awarded the Nobel Peace Prize for a steadfast dedication to non-violence. He has been criticised more recently because he does not want independence for Tibet; instead he wants it to remain a part of China but operate with its own rule. This type of rule is called autonomy.

The Dalai Lama says:	China says:
Tibet was independent and has been colonised.	Its reign over Tibet goes back over centuries.
Tibet should include neighbouring provinces with Tibetan populations.	It considers Tibet to be the Tibetan Autonomous Region only.
1.2 million people have been killed under Chinese rule.	It disputes the death toll.
China actively suppressed Tibetan identity.	It acknowledges some abuses but says it is helping the revival of Tibetan culture.
Recent development has favoured Han Chinese immigrants over the Tibetan people.	It says it has brought improvements in health and the economy.
The Tibetan cause has won the sympathy of individuals and groups, many of whom campaign for an independent Tibet.	No country openly disputes China's claim to sovereignty, and China has blocked all UN resolutions on Tibet.

March 2008 protests

In March 2008 Tibet erupted in protest following the 49th anniversary of the Tibetan Uprising of 1959. Chinese crackdowns on protesters resulted in the reported deaths of a hundred people, and highlighted the fact that China's record on human rights and freedoms remains one of the worst in the world. As the Beijing Olympics approached, the international news media joined human rights groups in condemning the Chinese occupation and suppression of Tibet, and called for the Olympics to be used to expose China's human rights abuses.

Collect a skill

Identifying points of view!

A key skill in Modern Studies is being able to identify differences of opinion.
Sometimes when you are asked to do this there will be lots of information and many differences. When this happens, look for the most extreme differences and focus on these.
Write down three differences of opinion between China and the Dalai Lama.

Show your understanding

1. Why does China have a poor record on human rights?
2. What do you think of the Dalai Lama? Discuss your answer with a partner.
3. What happened in March 2008?
4. There are lots of human rights being breached in Tibet. Use page 56 to help you identify them.

REVIEW

You have been asked to write a brief summary of what is happening in Tibet for your school website. However, you have been given only a small space on the Modern Studies page and so you have to explain the situation in less than 50 words!

39 What is the One Child Policy?

By the end of this section you should be able to:

▶ Explain why the One Child Policy was introduced
▶ Describe what the One Child Policy is
▶ Discuss the problems that the One Child Policy has caused

Why was China's population a problem?

China's population has grown significantly in the last 60 years. In 1950 China's population was approximately 560 million. Today the population stands at over 1.3 billion. The population of the whole world is roughly 6.7 billion, which means that China is home to a fifth of the world's people.

In the 1970's China's population was growing so fast that its people were starving. The Chinese government decided that something needed to be done about the growing population and so in 1979 China introduced a policy to try and stop its population from growing out of control.

 Activate your brain cells!

Imagine you were the leader of China in the 1970s. What would you have done about the population problem?

What is the One Child Policy?

The One Child Policy limits couples to having only one child. The policy was designed as a temporary measure but although it has been relaxed in some areas, it is still in place today.

Key features of the policy include:

- contraception widely available
- abortion available at any stage of pregnancy right up to birth
- only married couples with a permit allowed to have a child
- national advertising to remind people that it is better to have only one child.

What problems have been caused by the One Child Policy?

One of the main problems with the One Child Policy is that Chinese families prefer boys because they keep the family name. Traditionally, most Chinese people worked on the land and needed help from their sons. In the countryside girls are known as 'maggots in the rice' because they cost money to feed and then they marry a young man and leave without paying anything back. When a couple marry in China the girl will traditionally go and live with her husband's family, leaving her own parents to look after themselves in old age. Although a lot of Chinese families today live in cities and no longer need a son to work on their farm, the traditional preference for boys still exists.

This bias has resulted in female babies being aborted or killed at birth (infanticide). Many others are abandoned or placed in orphanages where they are left to die. There is now a gender imbalance in China's population, with approximately 120 boys for every 100 girls.

China's One Child Policy has created lots of spoiled only children, often called 'Little Emperors'

Other problems are caused by the way Chinese women have been treated since the policy was introduced in 1979. There have been reports of young women who were having routine operations being sterilised without their consent. Single, pregnant women have been forced to have an abortion and tortured. Families of women who had an unauthorised baby have also been tortured. Children born without a permit have been refused a name, a passport or an education. The One Child Policy breaches basic human rights by preventing an individual from choosing the size of their family.

Collect a skill

Support with evidence!

> The One Child Policy has been a success.

This is the view of a Chinese government spokesperson. Do you agree with the Chinese government spokesperson? Provide evidence to support your answer.

Show your understanding

1. Why did China introduce the One Child Policy?
2. Name two key features of the One Child Policy.
3. Why do Chinese families traditionally favour boys?
4. Describe three problems caused by the One Child Policy.
5. Imagine a society where there are a lot more males than females. Can you think of any problems that might occur?

What has the Chinese government done?

In 2004 the Chinese government introduced a programme called Girl Care. This was designed to encourage families to keep their girl babies and value them as much as boys. As a result, households with girls do not have to pay school fees; they also get preferential treatment in relation to housing, health care and employment. Couples with girls will also get a guaranteed pension when they retire.

REVIEW

Draw a memory map to summarise what you have learnt about the One Child Policy. If you need help with drawing a memory map then turn to page 63 and read **Collect a skill – Memory mapping!**

40 How does the Chinese political system work?

What are we exploring?

By the end of this section you should be able to:

▶ Explain what a one-party state is

▶ Identify the most powerful people in China

▶ Discuss how the Chinese political system operates

What is a one-party state?

China is very different from the United Kingdom. Only one political party is allowed to run the country: the Communist Party of China (CPC). This means that other groups or parties are not allowed to challenge the government in any way.

In the UK we have lots of different political parties. For example, the Conservatives, Labour, the Liberal Democrats, the SNP and Plaid Cymru. This means that people in the UK have a lot of choice and can influence those who make decisions about the country. In China there is only one choice – the CPC!

 Activate your brain cells!

Imagine there was only one political party in Scotland. What benefits and what problems do you think this would bring?

The Communist Party of China

The CPC was founded in 1921. It is the most powerful organisation in China. In 2009 it had over 73 million members. It is the largest political party in the world but it still only permits 5 per cent of the population to be members of the party.

This is so that the party membership remains something special; something which is only available to the **elite** members of society. An individual can apply for membership at eighteen years of age. Membership of the CPC is said to 'open doors' in China. This means that the members of the CPC get special treatment when it comes to employment, education, health care and housing.

Elite the richest, most powerful, best educated or most highly trained group in a society.

The aims of the CPC are:

• To uphold the communist line.

• To seek truth.

• To serve the people.

• To respect the hierarchy of the party structure.

The General Secretary of the CPC is a very powerful position in China. At present this position is held by Hu Jintao. He is also the President of China. China also has a Prime Minister and this role is held by Wen Jiabao. The President and the Prime Minister are both members of the CPC. The President is the head of state. This means he is responsible for China's foreign affairs. As General Secretary of the party he makes decisions about what the CPC stands for. The Prime Minister is the official head of the government and he runs the country.

China's political system is very different from ours. The main decision-making body in China is the Politburo. This is made up of 24 CPC officials and is elected by the party's central committee. Within the Politburo is the nine-member Standing Committee. This is the most powerful group of people in China. The way it operates is secret and the rest of the world is unclear as to how decisions are made inside the Standing Committee. China's Parliament is called the National People's Congress. It is supposed to be the most powerful organ of the Chinese government but it only meets once a year.

Is there any opposition to the CPC?

The CPC does not allow opposition in China. There are eight minor political parties but they do not have much power and are all connected to the CPC in some way. When people speak up against the CPC and the government they can be harassed, imprisoned and even tortured. Some groups that have tried to speak up against the CPC include Tiananmen Mothers, the Chinese Democracy Party, and the organisation Free Tibet.

Hu Jintao

Wen Jiabao

Show your understanding

1. What is a one-party state?
2. Make a factfile about the CPC. Include the following information: **Leader, When the party was founded, Aims, Logo, Number of members.**
3. What is the difference between the Prime Minister and the President in China?
4. What is the main decision-making body in China?
5. How often does the Chinese Parliament meet?
6. Is there opposition to the CPC in China?

REVIEW

The people of China have great political freedoms.

This is the view of a CPC official. Do you agree with the CPC official? Give reasons for your answer.

41 What challenges does China face in the future?

Activate your brain cells!

Think about it! Before you look at the challenges facing China, think about the challenges facing Scotland. Make a list and see how they compare!

Energy

It could be argued that China is fast becoming the world's most powerful country. It has the largest population at 1.3 billion (2008 estimate) and is estimated to become the largest economy by 2030. One challenge facing China is how to provide energy for such a large population.

As China's economy grows it results in road construction, airport building, increased industrial production and a greater demand for energy. China opened 47 new airports between 1990 and 2002, and its road network grew by 800,000 km from 1981 to 2002. More and more urban households are likely to adopt a western lifestyle, complete with air-conditioning, refrigerators, television sets, computers and other appliances.

At present most of China's energy is produced by burning coal. Coal is a fossil fuel, which means that burning it releases carbon and other harmful gases into the environment. China does want to increase the role of wind, biomass, hydro-electric and nuclear power but it will still rely heavily on coal.

China is increasingly coming under pressure from the rest of the world to reduce its carbon emissions. China is the world's biggest producer of CO_2 gases. However, a report in the *Guardian* newspaper recently revealed that more than half of China's recent rise in CO_2 emissions is created by manufacturing products for rich, developed countries including the United Kingdom. China is not willing to accept responsibility for CO_2 emissions produced when manufacturing goods for other countries. The argument over this issue will increase in the future as the effects of climate change worsen.

This is not a poor quality photograph – this is the smog in Beijing

Pollution and environmental damage

Another challenge facing China in the future is connected to the growing economy and to energy production, pollution and environmental damage. The speed of industrialisation and the growth of China's economy have been so fast that there have been dramatic effects on the environment and on the health of China's people. Pollution is now so bad that cancer is the leading cause of death in China. Air pollution alone is blamed for hundreds of thousands of deaths each year and nearly 500 million people lack access to safe drinking water.

During the 2008 Olympic Games much attention was paid to China's smog – the thick, dirty fog-like pollution that hangs over cities, making it difficult to breathe. It is estimated that only 1 per cent of China's urban population breathe air that would be considered safe by the European Union. Just weeks before the Games' opening ceremony in Beijing, planners had to implement an emergency plan to reduce the air pollution in the city. The measures they took to reduce air pollution included banning half of the city's cars, halting all construction work and closing factories for miles around the city. Obviously this is not a long-term solution and now that the Games are finished pollution continues to be a major problem.

Show your understanding

1. What evidence is there in the text of an increasing demand for energy?
2. How does China produce energy at the moment?
3. What evidence is there in the text that pollution causes health problems?
4. How did the Olympic Games' planners deal with the smog around Beijing before the event?

Collect a skill

Support with evidence!

It could be argued that China is not totally responsible for its increasing CO_2 emissions.

This is the view of a Chinese environmentalist. Do you agree with the Chinese environmentalist? Provide evidence to support your answer.

Stretch yourself

Energy production and pollution are not the only problems that China will face in the future. China still comes under heavy criticism for its human rights record. Use www.amnesty.org and www.hrw.org to find out more about China's human rights abuses. You can also use news websites like www.bbc.co.uk and www.guardian.co.uk.

Write a short report about human rights in China. Reports are based on facts and have sub-headings to explain what is in each section.

REVIEW

Now that you have learnt about some of the challenges facing China, how do you think these compare with the challenges facing Scotland? Can you think of any solutions to China's future challenges?

What are international problems?

What are we exploring?

By the end of this section you should be able to:
▶ Explain why some problems cross over the borders of countries
▶ Explain what makes these kinds of problems difficult to solve

There are many problems and issues that do not just affect one country but cross many countries and even the whole world. These are known as international problems.

Activate your brain cells!

Before reading any further ahead, discuss this idea with a partner and write a list of the kind of problems that might be considered international.

International problems are more significant and alarming in the modern world because we know about them in much more detail. News is broadcast around the world in real time. Journalists today do not have to wait until they get back to their desks to report their stories; they can email them straight to their editors from smartphones and laptops on site.

Some websites, like the BBC, are updated every few seconds by a team of journalists who are based all over the world; in war zones, in politically volatile countries, in major world powers, in places of interest and in places where disasters strike. This means that today's generation are much more aware of where in the world there are problems and of how bad things really are.

Why are international problems difficult to deal with?

International problems are extremely difficult to deal with because countries that normally do not work together need to co-operate in order to tackle them. Dealing with problems that cross borders is one of the biggest challenges that we will face in future generations. Three of the world's worst international problems are poverty, terrorism and climate change.

Each of these problems has an impact across the world in many countries and cannot be dealt with on a small scale within the borders of individual countries. So how do we deal with international problems?

There are many different theories about the best way to deal with the problems of terrorism, poverty and climate change but most people agree that countries need to work together to tackle them effectively.

International alliances are formed when countries join together with a common purpose. The largest international alliance is the UN.

Factfile: United Nations (UN)
Formed: 24 October 1945
Number of countries: 192
Aims:

- To maintain international peace and security.
- To develop friendly relations among nations.

- To co-operate in solving international problems and in promoting respect for human rights.
- To be a centre for regulating the actions of nations.

Source: www.un.org/Overview/uninbrief/about.shtml

The United Kingdom is also in the international alliance NATO.

Factfile: North Atlantic Treaty Organisation (NATO)
Formed: 4 April 1949
Number of countries: 28

Aims:
- To safeguard the freedom and security of its member countries by political and military means.
Source: www.nato.int

NATO members

The United Kingdom is also a member of the European Union (EU). The EU was formed originally as an economic organisation aimed at rebuilding Europe after the destruction of the Second World War, but today it is about much more than just money.

42 What are international problems? (cont.)

Factfile: The European Union (EU)

Formed: 9 May 1950

Number of countries: 27

Aims:

- To provide peace, prosperity and stability for its peoples.
- To overcome the divisions on the continent.
- To promote balanced economic and social development.
- To meet the challenges of globalisation and preserve the diversity of the peoples of Europe.
- To uphold the values that Europeans share, such as sustainable development and a sound environment, respect for human rights and the social market economy.

Source: www.europa.eu/index_en.htm

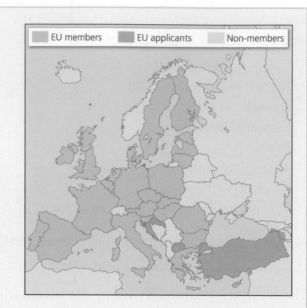

EU members   EU applicants   Non-members

As well as international alliances, Britain tries to tackle world problems in other ways. Britain is one of the G8 countries. The G8 includes Italy, Russia, Germany, France, Japan, UK, USA and Canada. This is an informal organisation of the seven leading industrialised countries plus Russia. The leaders of the G8 meet once a year to discuss global challenges. The G8 group is the target for a lot of criticism because there is often no action as a result of their meetings. In 2005 the G8 met in Gleneagles in Scotland. Tony Blair was hosting the meeting and so the UK was allowed to decide which topics would be on the agenda.

Learning link

Why is poverty an international problem?

Other examples of international organisations that attempt to deal with large-scale problems include the World Bank and the International Monetary Fund (IMF).

Many people feel that countries do not have a very good success rate in reaching agreements and so think that Non-Governmental Organisations (NGOs) like Oxfam and the Red Cross have a better chance of dealing with international problems.

Show your understanding

1. Why are some problems 'too big' for individual countries to solve?
2. What makes international problems difficult to deal with?
3. Why do countries want to be a part of the UN?
4. What type of methods does NATO use to protect the freedom and security of its member countries?
5. What are the aims of the EU?
6. Apart from the UN, NATO and the EU, are there other ways of trying to tackle international problems?

REVIEW

Design a classroom poster about the three main international alliances of which the UK is a member. Remember that classroom posters should be colourful, interesting to look at and contain important information!

43 What is poverty?

By the end of this section you should be able to:

▶ Explain what poverty is
▶ Describe the effects of poverty

In 2005 Bob Geldof, Bono and many other celebrities started a big campaign against world poverty. The Make Poverty History campaign focused on the G8 meeting in Gleneagles and was designed to put pressure on the world's most powerful countries to deal with poverty. On Saturday 2 July 2005, concerts took place in ten cities around the world starring 150 bands and 1250 musicians. The event was called Live8 and it was watched by an estimated three billion worldwide. After the summit the G8 leaders made many promises and there has been some very good progress in meeting these promises but poverty has not yet been made history.

 Activate your brain cells!

What do you already know about poverty? Discuss with a partner.

What is poverty?

There are many different definitions of poverty but the key to understanding it is knowing the difference between need and want. Need is something that is required in order to meet basic standards of living, such as water, food and shelter. Want is something that is not necessary for survival but that you may feel strongly about. You may want pizza for dinner but if you were starving and hadn't eaten in days all you would need would be bread and water.

Often on the news we hear about the growth of poverty in Scotland but this is different from the parts of the world where people die from poverty. A family living in poverty in Scotland may not be able to afford to heat their home properly in the winter or may not afford new clothes. A family living in poverty in India may not have four walls and a roof to keep out bad weather; they may not have shoes and they most likely will not have access to fresh running water or a toilet that flushes.

What kind of problems does poverty cause?

People die from poverty. During the Make Poverty History campaign there were television adverts with celebrities like Brad Pitt, Kylie Minogue and David Beckham snapping their fingers every three seconds. This was to symbolise the fact that one child dies from extreme poverty every three seconds.

Other problems which affect those living in poverty include HIV/AIDs, tuberculosis, lack of education, debt, substandard housing, poor government, human rights abuses, natural disasters and more. But why is poverty an international problem?

Malaria
Malaria is a disease spread by infected mosquitoes. More than one million people die from malaria every year. Malaria can be treated using anti-malarial drugs but these are expensive and are often not available in the countries where malaria is worst (approximately 80 per cent of malaria cases are found in African countries). The spread of malaria can be significantly reduced by mosquito nets. These are placed over a bed to protect people from mosquitoes (which come out at night) while they sleep. Nets are not expensive – about $6 – but this is still far too expensive for most families living in poverty.

Hunger and Famine
The most obvious problems caused by poverty are hunger and famine. Food is a basic need. According to the UN approximately 840 million people suffer from hunger and 34,000 children die from hunger every day. The problem is that poverty causes hunger; people cannot afford to buy enough food. People get weaker and become sick so they cannot work and are even less able to buy food and look after themselves and their families.

Sanitation system for taking dirty water and other sewage away from buildings and people's homes.

Collect a skill

Memory mapping!

Learning how to draw memory maps will help you in a lot of your school subjects. Memory mapping is a method you can use to help you organise your thoughts. Draw a memory map to show the effects of poverty. If you need help remembering how to draw a memory map look at page 63.

Diarrhoea
Another killer of those living in poverty is diarrhoea. Diarrhoea in Scotland is unpleasant and can result in a day or two off school but it doesn't kill. In developing countries diarrhoea is caused by a lack of access to clean water, lack of **sanitation** or poor hygiene. About 1.6 million people die of diarrhoea every year. In truth, they actually die of dehydration because they lose so much water along with vital salts. There is a very simple treatment which is very cheap: a mixture of sugar, salt and water. The problem is that because of poverty people do not have access to clean water for the treatment.

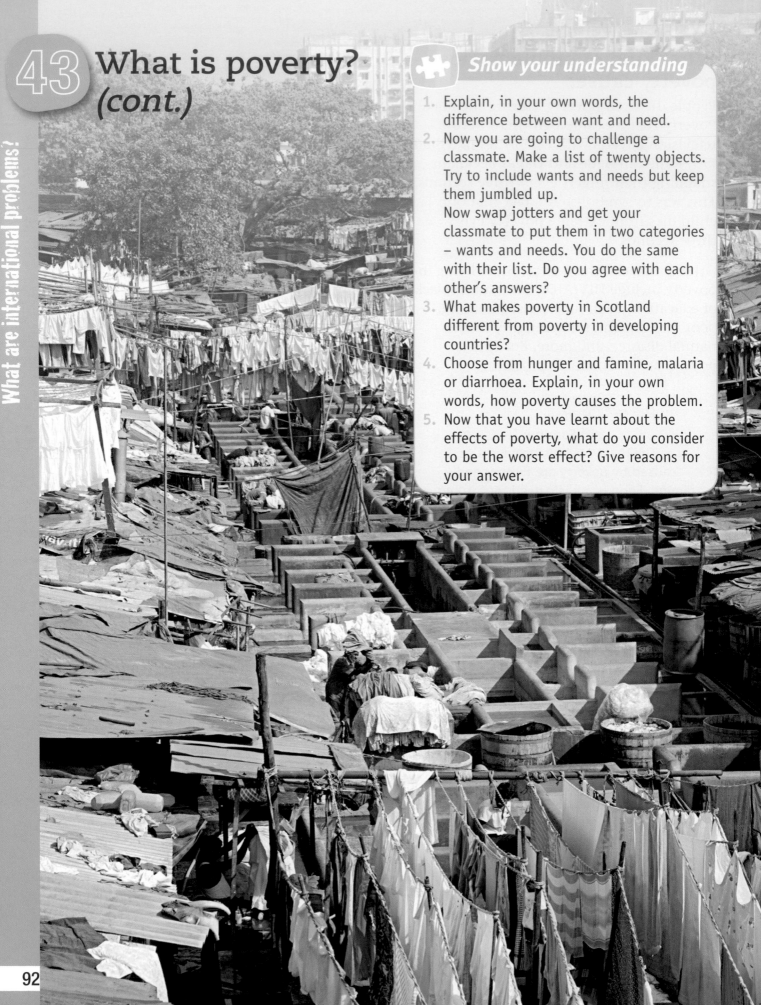

43 What is poverty? (cont.)

Show your understanding

1. Explain, in your own words, the difference between want and need.

2. Now you are going to challenge a classmate. Make a list of twenty objects. Try to include wants and needs but keep them jumbled up.
Now swap jotters and get your classmate to put them in two categories – wants and needs. You do the same with their list. Do you agree with each other's answers?

3. What makes poverty in Scotland different from poverty in developing countries?

4. Choose from hunger and famine, malaria or diarrhoea. Explain, in your own words, how poverty causes the problem.

5. Now that you have learnt about the effects of poverty, what do you consider to be the worst effect? Give reasons for your answer.

In the year 2000 the UN came up with eight goals for development.

Eradicate extreme poverty and hunger	Improve maternal health care
Achieve universal primary education	Combat HIV/AIDs, malaria and other diseases
Promote gender equality and empower women	Ensure environmental sustainability
Reduce child mortality	Develop a goal partnership for development

The goals were known as the Millennium Development Goals and they were agreed upon by almost all of the world's countries. The target for completion is 2015. In some countries there has been a lot of progress in trying to meet the goals but in other countries things have got worse. There is a worry that the global economic crisis will have a large negative effect on the progress.

 Show your understanding

Choose three of the Millennium Development Goals and explain why you think they are important

? Bore your friends ...

On 2 July 2005 more than 225,000 people formed a huge white human band around the centre of Edinburgh as part of the Make Poverty History campaign.

Why is poverty an international problem?

By the end of this section you should be able to:
► Explain why poverty is an international problem
► Describe what the UK government does to help people in poverty
► Describe an aid project

More than 1 billion people in the world's poorest countries live on less than $1 a day. This is an international problem because the scale of the poverty is so huge. The countries where poverty is at its worst are not able to deal with it on their own because they are so poor. They need help and support from the rest of the world.

The problem is that the countries of the world who can afford to help have other priorities. All countries face challenges and problems such as paying for education, health care, looking after their own poor people and defending themselves. This is why campaigns like Make Poverty History try to remind the world of how bad the lives of the world's poor really are.

What does the UK do?

The UK government department dedicated to helping the world's developing countries is the Department for International Development (DFID). DFID believes that 'many of the problems which affect us – war and conflict, international crime, refugees, the trade in illegal drugs and the spread of diseases like HIV and AIDS – are caused or made worse by poverty in developing countries. Getting rid of poverty will make for a better world for everybody.' (Source: www.dfid.gov.uk)

DFID gives aid directly to poor countries and works with international organisations such as the UN and the World Bank, as well as NGOs like the Red Cross and Oxfam.

How do people help?

Countries and organisations try to help poorer developing countries through aid projects.

Aid Project 1

Organisation: DFID and UNICEF (United Nations International Children's Emergency Fund)

Where: Malawi

Population: 13.1 million

Average Life Expectancy: 39 years

Total UK aid received 2007/2008: £72.6 million

The project: When Malawi cancelled school fees in 1994 the schools became overcrowded and the buildings could not cope. DFID, along with UNICEF, have been working in Malawi to improve toilet facilities in schools like M'buka. As well as providing the improved facilities, the organisations also gave lessons on good hygiene. The aim was to raise healthier children who were better able to learn.

Success: At M'buka alone, the new facilities have made a major difference. As 12-year-old pupil Edna Phiri testifies:

'Since the urinals were built, I've been attending school regularly. Also, I don't have to go to the bush to urinate, as I did before. In fact, there are fewer girls getting sick – before the toilets were built, you sometimes stepped in faeces on your way to the bush.'

(Source: http://www.dfid.gov.uk/casestudies/files/africa/malawi-girls-urinals.asp)

Aid Project 2

Organisation: DFID

Where: Ghana

Population: 22.9 million

Average Life Expectancy: 59 years

Total UK aid received 2007/2008: £93 million

The project: Thanks to a £250,000 grant from DFID and supermarket Waitrose, a company called Akwaaba is about to be launched in Ghana. This will produce exotic fruit juices and smoothies using Ghana's local produce.

Success: Approximately 5 per cent of Akwaaba's profits will go to the Blue Skies Foundation, which aims to improve the lives of farm workers and their communities by investing in social and economic projects. These will help local people with education, housing, health care, sanitation and employment.

(Source: www.dfid.gov.uk/media-room/case-studies/2009/helping-ghanas-fruit-producers-enter-juicy-uk-market/)

 Show your understanding

1. Why is poverty an international problem?
2. What is DFID?
3. Why does DFID help poorer countries?
4. How will Aid Project 1 help the people of Malawi?
5. What is the life expectancy in Malawi? Can you think of any reasons for this?
6. What is Aid Project 2 trying to do?
7. Which supermarket chain is involved in Aid Project 2?

What is climate change?

What are we exploring?

By the end of this section you should be able to:

▶ Explain what climate change is

▶ Explain how climate change will affect humans

▶ Explain how climate change will affect nature

Climate change is a very controversial subject. Many people believe that it is the biggest challenge facing the human population in the future.

 Activate your brain cells!

What do you already know about climate change? Work with a partner and draw a memory map to summarise what you know.

What is climate change?

Throughout the earth's lifetime its climate has been through many changes brought on by natural causes, but since the early twentieth century the temperature of the earth has risen dramatically.

This global warming is what we now refer to as climate change. The cause of this global warming is thought to be largely due to human activity. The greenhouse effect is a natural phenomenon that keeps the world warm, but over the last 150 years humans have been pumping more and more CO_2 into the atmosphere, causing the greenhouse effect to strengthen and resulting in global warming.

So what?

The problem is that this dramatic rise in temperature across the globe has resulted in numerous side-effects which are going to have an increasingly large impact on us in years to come.

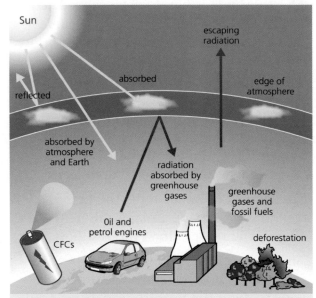

The greenhouse effect

One of the most well-known effects of climate change is on water. Approximately 75 per cent of the world's fresh water is held in glaciers and ice sheets. As the temperature increases the ice melts. This has several knock-on effects. Around the world sea levels are predicted to rise. Estimates of how much they will rise vary enormously; a low estimate predicts a rise of 0.9 m by 2100. This would mean millions of people all over the world would be made homeless. In Bangladesh alone, 6 million people live less than one metre above sea level.

The weather we experience in Britain would also see changes. You may think that an increase in temperature sounds like a good thing – more sunbathing, more dry football matches, fewer cold winters. However, the reality is predicted to be very different. An increase in storms is predicted, both in strength and numbers. Storm surges are predicted to cause more coastal flooding. Flooding in Britain is likely to become much more common as rainfall becomes more extreme, especially in the summer months. Extended dry spells will also cause many problems throughout the UK – crops will fail, farmers will have to change what they grow to suit altered growing seasons, droughts will cause water shortages, numbers of hot-weather deaths will increase, and cases of skin cancer will increase. Malaria could even spread to some areas of the UK.

As weather patterns change across the world so, too, will the plants and animals that can survive. Scientists are concerned that species which are already endangered could die out completely and that many animals and plants may disappear from the world altogether. Some species will be able to adapt quickly, moving to find new habitats in suitable climates, but others will not and could face extinction. Plant and animal species have had to adapt before to climate change, such as during the Ice Age, so they may cope better than scientists predict. However, it is likely that these changes may happen too fast.

Show your understanding

1. What is the greenhouse effect? Include a diagram in your answer.
2. How will climate change affect sea levels?
3. Are scientists concerned about how nature will cope with climate change? Why?
4. Visit the government's information site www.direct.gov.uk and find out more about the effects of climate change. Use the search facility on the site and type in 'climate change'.
   Now choose whether to write a report, make a PowerPoint® presentation or design a webpage about the effects of climate change.

Collect a skill

Identify exaggeration!

> *Our weather in Scotland will get hotter and sunnier. I am looking forward to climate change.*

This is the view of Fiona White. Can Fiona be accused of exaggeration? Give reasons for your answer.

REVIEW

Describe, in your own words, what is meant by climate change.

46 Why is climate change an international problem?

What are we exploring?

By the end of this section you should be able to:

▶ Explain why climate change cannot be dealt with unless countries work together

▶ Explain some of the barriers to countries working together

▶ Describe what you can do to reduce climate change

Since climate change is thought to be connected to emissions of greenhouse gases it is truly a global problem. One country's emissions have an impact not only on their own people and wildlife but they contribute to climate change across the world. This becomes even more complicated because it is the poorest countries in the world that are likely to suffer most from the effects of climate change, but it is the richest countries who are to blame. The richest countries in the world are the ones who created the initial problem by pumping out masses of CO_2 when they became industrialised in the nineteenth and early twentieth centuries. Today the poorer countries are industrialising and are now contributing to greenhouse gases.

What is happening?

One of the biggest challenges now is to reach a new agreement following the end of the Kyoto Protocol in 2012. The Kyoto Protocol was an agreement written after a **summit** in Japan in 1997. The Protocol did not become law until 2005 because so many countries argued over its contents. The USA and Australia did not agree to the Protocol because it did not expect poor developing countries to meet the same emissions standards as developed countries.

Summit an important meeting of leaders from two or more countries.

Now it is time for a new agreement and countries are still arguing.

The UN, EU and G8 are working to try to reach an agreement with other countries around the world. Progress is being made but a new agreement is going to be difficult. The most recent report from the Intergovernmental Panel on Climate Change states that action must be taken quickly to reduce emissions. The consequences of climate change are becoming more severe.

What can be done to reduce emissions?

The most obvious method of reducing emissions is to stop using fossil fuels. Fossil fuels are coal, gas and oil. They were formed millions of years ago under the ground and once they have been used they cannot be replaced. Fossil fuels are therefore also known as non-renewable resources. When fossil fuels are burned carbon is released into the atmosphere.

Fossil fuels in the UK are mainly used for the creation of electricity, so using alternative energy is the main way emissions can be reduced. Wind farms, marine (tidal and wave) power, and solar and hydro-electric power are all alternative ways of producing electricity. Both the Scottish and UK

governments state that they are committed to increasing the number of alternative energy projects in coming years.

What can you do?

As well as large-scale projects there is a lot that can be done by individuals and families.

Save energy and water at home:

Turn down your thermostat.

Improve insulation in your home.

Use energy-saving light bulbs.

Shorten the time spent in the shower.

Only fill the kettle with the amount of water that you need.

Turn lights off when you are not using them.

Do not leave electrical equipment on standby.

The energy you use at home is likely to be your biggest contribution to climate change. 80 per cent of energy used at home goes on heating and hot water.

Reuse and recycle:

Avoid waste by repairing items instead of discarding them.

Recycle as much as you can.

Compost all fruit and vegetable waste. Reusing and recycling means that fewer products are being made and less energy is being wasted.

Use public transport:

This is an easy one for you because you can't drive yet. Cycle, walk or use public transport wherever you can. Car fumes account for 25 per cent of emissions from individuals.

Shop 'green':

Avoid using supermarket disposable bags – take your own.

Avoid products with lots of packaging.

Buy local produce that hasn't needed to be transported over a large distance.

Buy recycled paper and glass products.

Transporting and packaging goods for supermarkets uses lots of energy.

 Show your understanding

1. Why can climate change not be dealt with by individual countries?
2. What is the Kyoto Protocol?
3. Why are poor countries not included in the Kyoto agreement?
4. What solutions to the problem are being used in the UK?
5. What are fossil fuels?
6. Give five examples of things you can do to help combat climate change.

Stretch yourself

How can you and your classmates make a difference to people's opinions on climate change? In a small group discuss things that have been done in the past and whether or not they have been successful. Come up with a plan for your school. How can you encourage parents and teachers to help?

REVIEW

Why do you think it is important to have an international agreement on climate change and emissions? Provide reasons for your answer.

47 How do I investigate?

One of the most important skills for anyone studying Modern Studies to learn is how to investigate. Once you know how to carry out an investigation you can find out about any topic you like and are interested in.

Step 1 Choosing a topic

Usually your teacher will tell you what topic you should investigate but sometimes you may be allowed to choose your own. A topic should always be something broad so that there is plenty to investigate, otherwise you will not be able to get enough information to write up a good investigation. Typical Modern Studies topics include things like The Elderly in Britain, USA Elections, Aid to Africa, Poverty in the UK, or the Success of the NHS.

For this investigation we will use the topic Human Rights in China.

Step 2 Writing a hypothesis

The next stage of carrying out an investigation is to write a hypothesis.

A hypothesis is a statement that you will either prove or disprove. For example, a very simple hypothesis about a class test would be that 'All the boys in the class will score higher marks than the girls'. This is very simple because at the end of the test it will be easy to prove it or disprove it. When carrying out an investigation you need your hypothesis to be more complicated so that there are lots of parts to investigate before you find out the answer.

Have a go at writing a hypothesis for the following topics. The first two have been done for you to help you get started.

Topic: Poverty in the USA

Hypothesis: Single-parent families are more likely to be poor than all other types of households.

Topic: The Elderly in the UK

Hypothesis: The UK government is not doing enough to meet the needs of elderly people.

Topic: The Scottish Parliament

Topic: The Rights of the Child

Topic: The Powers of the Police

Your teacher may give you different topics that you have studied in class.

Now write a hypothesis for our topic: Human Rights in China.

Step 3 Writing aims

The next stage of the investigation process is very important. Writing aims helps you break down your investigation into bite-size chunks so that it is easier for you to carry out.

Each aim should be a short statement or a question that will help you answer your hypothesis. Aims can be written in two ways: either as a question or as a statement beginning with 'To find out ...'

So far you have chosen the topic Human Rights in China and you have written your hypothesis, such as 'China has a poor record on human rights'. Below are four aims that could be used for this investigation.

Aim 1: To find out what rights are protected by law in China.

Aim 2: To find out if Amnesty International has reported on human rights problems in China.

Aim 3: To find out if Human Rights Watch has reported on human rights problems in China.

Aim 4: To find out in detail about one example of human rights abuse in China.

Now rewrite these aims as questions. The first one has been done for you.

Aim 1: What rights are protected by law in China?

Aim 2:

Aim 3:

Aim 4:

Step 4 Methodology

To complete Step 4 you are going to plan which methods you will use to achieve your aims. There are many different methods that Modern Studies students can use to investigate, and each one has advantages and disadvantages.

Television

There are lots of different ways to learn from television programmes.

In Modern Studies we use:

- documentaries, e.g. *The Zimmers*
- news programmes, e.g. BBC News
- politics programmes, e.g. *Question Time*
- drama, e.g. *Britz*
- films, e.g. *Blood Diamond*.

There are laws to govern television programmes so that they must not be biased or exaggerated. The problem with TV programmes is that sometimes we can think they are real when they are actually fictional. Also, they can quickly become out of date.

47 How do I investigate? (cont.)

Internet

We also use the Internet to find out about the topics we study in Modern Studies.

This is a quick and easy way of finding information but it can also cause confusion, as sometimes there is too much information. We use search engines like Google™ to help us find what we are looking for by typing in keywords. For example, if we wanted to find out about the Scottish Parliament we would type in 'Scottish Parliament' as our keywords.

Books

Many books provide detailed information for Modern Studies. Some books are specifically written for Modern Studies, such as books about politics or society. Encyclopaedias are also very useful as they contain information about lots of different issues. Books are easy to use and your local librarian can help you to find what you are looking for. However, books go out of date very quickly.

Surveys

A survey is a list of questions on a specific topic. For example, if you wanted to find out the most popular football teams in your school you could conduct a survey to find the answers. Surveys provide very up-to-

date information and can be done on any topic you want. The problem with surveys is that they can take a long time and you can end up with too much data to process.

Learning link

How do I carrry out a survey?

Writing letters

This is another way of finding out information. For example, you could write to your local MSP. Writing letters is a good method to use because you can ask direct questions, but some people are very busy and might not find time to write back. You might have to wait a long time for a reply. One of the main problems is that you have to know who to write to in the first place.

Sending emails

The biggest advantage of using email is that you can communicate with people from all over the world instantly. Busy people are more likely to answer an email than a letter. Email is easy to use and free. The problems with email are that you have to know who to contact and not everyone has access to the Internet.

Step 5 Carrying out your research

Now you are ready to carry out research. Your methodology is your plan for how to do this. The simplest way to keep a record of your research is to write each aim at the top of a piece of paper and then make notes under the relevant aim. Make sure you keep track of where you find your information – note down the website or book and page number next to your notes.

When you are happy that you have enough information to answer each aim, read through them carefully. You are now ready to rewrite your notes into your own words. This is the most difficult part of an investigation. You need to make sure you understand the information you have collected before you can write your answers. Some information may be too difficult to understand. Do not worry about ditching information at this stage. Just because you collected the information does not mean it will make a good investigation. If there is something you don't understand, get rid of it.

At the end of each aim you should have a clear answer – a mini-conclusion.

Step 6 Presenting your investigation

Investigations can be presented in many different ways: as a poster, as a PowerPoint® presentation, as a video/YouTube clip or as a booklet.

Your investigation should include the following:

- Title (Topic and Hypothesis)
- Aims
- Methodology
- Answer to each aim
- Conclusion
- List of sources

Discuss with your teacher which method of presentation you are going to use. Now use the information you collected in Step 5 and present your investigation.

Step 7 Writing a conclusion

Your conclusion should summarise each of your aim answers and bring them together to answer your hypothesis. You should clearly state whether you have proved or disproved your hypothesis.

Now write your conclusion.

Step 8 Sources

Your final step is to list all of your information sources. This is called referencing. You must not use other people's information without referencing it. Even if you got your information from an interview with your mum, you should note down your mum's name, the date and the time of your interview.

Now write your source list

Congratulations – you have now completed a Modern Studies Investigation!

What's the big deal with chewing gum?

What are we exploring?

By the end of this section you should be able to:
▶ Identify and give examples of the four main types of industry
▶ Speak about the history of chewing gum

Chewing gum is said to be the world's most common habit and about 100,000 tonnes of gum are consumed every year. Most of us are familiar with the negative aspects of chewing gum – when we find it on chairs, stuck under desks or on our shoes. However, there are also many benefits of chewing gum and it is big business!

 Activate your brain cells!

- Can you work out approximately how many bits of chewing gum you have chewed in your life? Share your results with your class and calculate your class total.
- Make a list of five reasons why people choose to chew gum.

Types of industry

Industry is the general word that we use to describe economic activity. Economic activity is work that people get paid for or voluntary work that improves the income of an organisation or company.

Industry is often divided into four areas:

Primary industry: gathering materials from the land or sea (e.g. farming, fishing or quarrying).

Secondary or manufacturing industry: making products into something to sell (e.g. building houses, assembling mobile phones or making furniture).

Tertiary or service industry: providing a service to other people (e.g. teaching, working in a shop or driving a bus).

Quaternary industry: cutting-edge research that makes use of modern technology (e.g. designing the latest smartphone, creating a new Internet search engine or working on a cure for malaria).

What type of industry is the chewing gum industry?

Actually it is all four types:

Primary products
The gum base

Chewing gum is traditionally made of chicle, a natural latex product that is harvested from trees and is also used in bicycle inner tubes. Chicle is still used in Japan but in most other countries a synthetic gum base is made from rubber and plastics. It is the gum base that puts the chew in chewing gum!

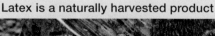
Latex is a naturally harvested product

Sweeteners

Powdered cane sugar, beet sugar and corn syrup are used in the production of sugar-sweetened chewing gums. All of these things have to be harvested.

Flavour

The most popular flavours for chewing gums come from the mint plant.

Natural mint

Secondary manufacturing process

The gum base is poured into a mixer and then colour, flavouring, softeners and preservatives are all added to the mix. As the gum is being mixed, sweeteners are also added. After about 30 minutes the gum is ready to be moulded into shapes. It is then cooled, chopped up into bite-size chunks and individually wrapped.

This whole process takes place in large mechanised factories as part of an assembly line.

The secondary manufacturing process

Tertiary selling process

Just like any product, chewing gum needs to be sold and this means that you need someone to sell it to you in the shops. As well as the retail assistants and shop owners there is a whole team of people working for big chewing gum companies to market and advertise the product and also to work out exclusive deals with retail chains.

Quaternary industry

Even though the actual process of making chewing gum hasn't really changed for 150 years, developing the next generation of 'super' gum could be big business. Companies like Wrigley spend millions of pounds every year on research and development. In 2009 some clever people even developed biodegradable chewing gum.

Show your understanding

1. How many tonnes of chewing gum have been consumed globally since you were born?
2. In your own words describe the four main types of industry.
3. Make your own version of the table below:

Primary	Secondary	Tertiary	Quarternary

Fill the table in by giving at least five examples of each type of industry.

4. Why do you think scientists are working to develop biodegradable chewing gum?

Why is Wrigley a global brand?

What are we exploring?

By the end of this section you should be able to:

▶ Describe what is meant by a global brand

▶ Understand the location factors of why factories are built in certain locations

▶ Explain what is meant by government aid

A little history

The William Wrigley Jr. Company was founded in Chicago in 1891. Originally it specialised in selling products such as soap and baking powder. Then in 1892 they started offering chewing gum with every can of baking powder that they sold. In the end, the chewing gum became more popular than the baking powder and Wrigley's chewing gum was born!

Wrigley's Gum – a global brand

Activate your brain cells!

- Wrigley is a brand. Working with a partner, how many other brands of chewing gum can you name?
- How many different flavours of chewing gum can you name? Start with the letter A, then B, then C etc. ... can you get a flavour for every letter of the alphabet?

A global brand

Wrigley really is a global brand – you will find its chewing gum in supermarkets, pharmacies and vending machines in over 180 countries worldwide.

It has fourteen factories as well as various offices and distribution centres around the world. The company employs about 16,000 people.

• Wrigley factories

Wrigley factories and offices around the globe

Where does Wrigley locate its factories?

Unlike primary industry that is always located near the source of its raw materials and the service industry that is often found in towns and cities where people live, deciding on the location of a chewing gum factory is a little bit harder. The following location factors need to be taken into account:

Government aid

Sometimes the governments of countries offer incentives such as grants, loans and tax breaks to encourage multinational companies to locate in certain areas.

This normally occurs in towns or cities where there are areas of high unemployment, or areas where other factories are about to close and new industrial development is needed.

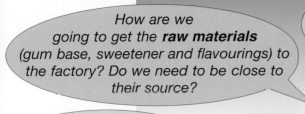

How are we going to get the **raw materials** (gum base, sweetener and flavourings) to the factory? Do we need to be close to their source?

Is there any **government aid** available?

Are there **good transport links** to import the raw materials and to export the gum?

What **skills do people need** to manufacture chewing gum?

Is the **market (customers)** nearby?

How will we **power our machines**? Is **green energy** available locally?

Is there an appropriate **labour supply** nearby?

Is there a factory that we could just hire or rent from within the host country?

Is there a **suitable site** to locate the factory? Is there **enough flat land** for expansion?

A family business?

Until recently, Wrigley has always been a family business and that is quite unusual for a company of its size. Just look at the list of Chief Executive Officers (CEOs) from over the years:

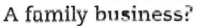

- **1891–1932** William Wrigley Jr.
- **1932–1961** Philip K. Wrigley
- **1961–1999** William Wrigley III
- **1999–2006** William Wrigley, Jr. II
- **2006–2008** William Perez
- **2008–present** Dushan 'Duke' Petrovich

What a lot of people don't know is that in 2008 Wrigley was bought by the Mars Corporation. This is a good example of globalisation; when larger multinational companies expand and take over smaller companies.

 Show your understanding

1. Why do you think Wrigley chewing gum became so popular?
2. Why do you think you can find chewing gum in a pharmacy?
3. Study the map on the page opposite.
   - Which continents do not have Wrigley factories and offices?
   - Using five bullet points, describe the location of Wrigley factories and offices around the world.
4. Look at the picture on this page.
   - Why do you think it would be beneficial for Wrigley factories to be near an airport? (Remember: it is a global brand.)
   - What do you think is meant by 'green energy'?
   - Write a song, rap or poem to help you remember the location factors.
5. Why do you think that Mars prefer people to think that Wrigley's Gum is still a family business?

50 How did the credit crunch affect the chewing gum industry?

What are we exploring?

By the end of this section you should be able to:

▶ Explain a little bit about the credit crunch (it's quite complicated!)

▶ Describe how the credit crunch affects people and business

What is a credit crunch?

Credit is normally a loan or an overdraft from a bank or building society. A credit crunch is a reduction in the availability of loans (or credit) from a bank. It may also include the sudden changing or tightening of the conditions that are required to get a loan from the lender.

For example, before the global credit crunch, if you wanted to buy a house you could borrow 100 per cent of the money (a mortgage) from your bank (as long as you were earning over a certain amount each year). Now, you can still get a mortgage but you will need a big deposit – it is now very difficult to borrow 100 per cent of the money you need to buy the property.

How did the credit crunch start?

It's complicated – very complicated – but basically in a number of MEDCs (More Economically Developed Countries), banks had lent far too much money to people who could not afford to repay the debt. Some of this money was for people to buy houses that were greatly overpriced. When the banks tried to repossess the houses from people, they still couldn't get their money

Activate your brain cells!

- How much do you think you would have to save as a deposit if you wanted to buy a house worth £100,000?
- How much do you think you would need to earn each year for the bank to lend you the money?
- Discuss your thoughts with your class. Your teacher will help you.

back because the houses weren't worth as much any more – the value of the houses had fallen.

The same sort of thing happened with credit cards. Banks allowed people to build up massive amounts of debt on their credit cards, but then people couldn't pay back the money. Banks couldn't get their money back because people just didn't have it.

So banks stopped giving credit and lots of people had to stop buying things. This becomes a cycle of depression:

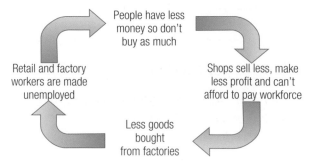

People have less money so don't buy as much

Shops sell less, make less profit and can't afford to pay workforce

Less goods bought from factories

Retail and factory workers are made unemployed

Did people chew less in the credit crunch?

Actually, it has been shown that sales of things like chewing gum remain the same or might even go up during a recession. One of the reasons for this is that people try to make other cost savings and one big cost saving is to try to give up smoking. Chewing gum has been proven to help people give up smoking.

People also try to look for ways to be more efficient. If a shop just sells small products (like chewing gum) it might be cheaper for the shop owner to replace one of their members of staff with a vending machine. This won't affect sales of the gum but is likely to increase profits.

Some chewing gum production in the Wrigley Plymouth factory was affected by the credit crunch (see the article below) but some experts think that this might have just been to try to get the workforce to behave more efficiently.

Show your understanding

1. Write your own definitions for the following words: **credit**, **mortgage**, **lender** and **overdraft**. If you are not sure, think about using a dictionary (an online one will do).
2. Make a cartoon strip to describe how the credit crunch started. If you don't want to make a cartoon strip, choose another way to present your work.
3. Make your own copy of the cycle of depression – use a bit of colour to make it look less depressing!
4. In your own words explain why chewing gum sales were not really affected by the credit crunch.
5. What do we mean by an efficiency saving?
6. What does Wrigley mean by a 'short-time working plan'?
7. Imagine that you worked for the Wrigley factory in Plymouth. Write a letter or an email to your boss explaining why you should keep your job.

Thursday, April 09, 2009   **The Plymouth Herald**

Wrigley tells 300 staff to stay at home

ONE of Plymouth's largest employers has told 300 of its 450 workers to stay at home today, as it introduces 'unfortunate' measures to fight the recession.

Manufacturing at the Wrigley Company plant ground to a halt for the day as part of a 'short-time working plan', the confectionery firm has announced.

Bosses at the famous chewing gum brand have revealed that the factory will also be shutting its doors for a four-day stint next month as Wrigley battles a drop in sales.

A Wrigley spokeswoman said: 'Many manufacturing operations have been affected by the current economic climate in the UK, and Wrigley, like others, is not immune to this – as consumers make fewer visits to the shops and travel less.

It's not about shutting anything down – we are in a difficult economic climate and many manu-

facturing operators have done the same thing by closing their factories down for a number of days.'

In January, Wrigley announced it may be cutting up to 16 jobs during a review of its 'operational structure', with a number of roles described as 'at risk'.

However, the firm insists it has no plans to relocate its Estover factory, or shut it down for good.

The Wrigley Company has been based in Plymouth for nearly 40 years and has made multi-million-pound investments in its facilities over that time.

? Bore your friends...

25 per cent of chewing gum produced in Plymouth is exported overseas.

Explore further

Have a look at how the 2008 credit crunch unfolded in pictures:

http://widerimage.reuters.com/timesofcrisis/

51 How is chewing gum advertised?

What are we exploring?

By the end of this section you should be able to:

▶ Describe how things are advertised

▶ Understand what we mean by consumerism

▶ Explain the difference between advertising and sponsorship

Advertising is a form of communication intended to persuade its viewers, readers or listeners to take some action. In commercial advertising this will normally involve buying a particular product. Modern advertising developed with the rise of mass production in the late nineteenth and early twentieth centuries.

 Activate your brain cells!

- Think about the last time you **watched television.** Do you remember any adverts? Which ones do you remember and why do you think you remember them?
- Think about the last time you **went online.** Do you remember any adverts? Which ones do you remember and why do you think you remember them?
- Think about the last time you **listened to the radio.** Do you remember any adverts? Which ones do you remember and why do you think you remember them?

Types of advertising

People advertise in lots of places including:

- newspapers
- magazines
- television
- radio
- billboards
- websites
- bus shelters

Consumerism

Consumerism is the idea that personal happiness can be obtained through consumption – the purchase of goods and services. Many advertisers rely on consumerism to sell as many of their products as possible. They create the illusion that people can't live without their products or services. Young people are particularly vulnerable to consumerism.

Advertisers aren't allowed to lie about what their products and services will bring to an individual (that would be illegal) but they

Large companies often try to improve their advertising through a brand. Wrigley is a chewing gum brand. When Mars bought Wrigley in 2008 it decided to keep the Wrigley brand because it was very strong. You wouldn't buy Mars chewing gum, would you?

do sometimes exaggerate. It is the job of the UK's Consumer Focus to keep an eye on exactly what companies say – if they exaggerate too much they may get a hefty fine, have to make a public apology, or even be banned from advertising their product.

Use of children in advertising

Some chewing gum companies try to make it really appealing for young people to chew gum. There are health benefits to chewing gum but, like anything, it has to be the right type of gum and it also has to be done in moderation.

Companies are keen to get children involved in their products from a young age as it means they are likely to use them for the rest of their lives. The majority of human beings are creatures of habit and don't normally change their consumer behaviour unless a completely revolutionary product comes along.

In order for products to be appealing to young people, they need to feature young people in their advertisements. This might be pictures on the Internet, video on the television or voices on the radio.

Some people think that under-eighteens should not be used to advertise commercial products for big multinational companies.

Advertising vs sponsorship

Show your understanding

1. Explain what we mean by advertising. Do this in the form of an advert (maybe a jingle?).
2. Why do you think you don't buy Mars chewing gum?
3. Think about an advert you've seen recently.
   - List two good things and two bad things that could be improved about the advert.
   - Make your own A6-sized chewing gum advert that could appear in a magazine.
4. Look at the list of types of advertising. Put the list into order of importance to you. The most effective form of advertising should go at the top of the list.
5. What is consumerism?
6. Why do you think it is important for organisations like the Consumer Focus to exist?
7. A new type of mobile phone (like the iPhone) is a good example of a revolutionary product. Can you name five other revolutionary products that you know about?
8. With a partner discuss whether you think children should be used in the advertising of chewing gum. See if you can argue both for and against the idea.
9. Why do you think that Wrigley sponsors:
   - Plymouth Raiders
   - World Rally Championships?
10. Make your own chewing gum advert to appear on the web, TV or radio. It should be at least 30 seconds long.

November 2008

Chewing Gum News

The Wrigley Company is pleased to announce that Airwaves is now the official chewing gum sponsor of the World Rally Championship and the main sponsor of local basketball team the Plymouth Raiders.

Wrigley Airwaves sponsors the World Rally Championship

Why can't you chew gum in Singapore?

What are we exploring?

By the end of this section you should be able to:

▶ Describe the location of Singapore and its main characteristics

▶ Explain why chewing gum was banned in Singapore

Singapore is an island city-state off the southern tip of the Malay Peninsula in South East Asia. It's about 135 km north of the equator. Singapore is classified as a microstate and is the smallest nation in South East Asia.

Although it is small, Singapore has evolved into one of the most developed countries in the world. Its main economy is based around the manufacturing industry and includes electronics, petroleum refining, chemicals, mechanical engineering and biomedical sciences.

It's a very crowded, busy place to live and work.

Brief history of Singapore

- **Pre 1819:** Various inhabitants since AD200, but the island was mainly inhabited by fishermen.
- **1819–1940:** Singapore was part of the British Empire.
- **1941–1945:** Singapore was occupied by the Japanese during the Second World War.
- **1945:** Britain repossessed the island a month after Japan surrendered from Second World War.
- **1955:** Singapore had its first general election.
- **1963:** Singapore declared independence from Britain and joined the Federation of Malaysia along with Malaya, Sabah and Sarawak.
- **1965:** Singapore left the Federation of Malaysia and officially gained sovereignty on 9 August 1965.

	Singapore	Compared to other countries
Area	710 km² (274 sq miles)	187th largest country
Population (2009)	4,987,600 people	115th most populated country
Population density	6,814 people/km²	3rd most densely populated country
GDP per capita	$56,226	4th richest country for GDP
Currency	Singapore dollar	–
Human development index (HDI)	0.944	23rd (very high)

The Singapore chewing gum ban

Chewing gum has been banned in Singapore since 1992. It is illegal for anyone to bring chewing gum into the country. The law did change slightly in 2004 to allow the importing of gum for therapeutic and medical reasons.

Why was gum banned?

Chewing gum was banned because the Prime Minister at the time (Goh Chok Tong) decided that people were being very irresponsible with their gum and it was costing the government a lot of money to clean up. It was being left on pavements, in keyholes, in post boxes, and under seats on public transport, and was damaging cleaning equipment – which cost the government even more money. The final straw was when Singapore opened its new metro system. Trains were sometimes delayed when people stuck gum on the sensors and this stopped the doors from closing.

Black market chewing gum

No real black market for chewing gum in Singapore has ever emerged. This is partly because when the ban was introduced, anyone caught bringing gum into the country was publicly named and shamed as a smuggler. Singapore also has some very strict laws and very severe punishments, which might be why it has such a low crime rate in general.

? Bore your friends ...

The Malay Peninsula includes Burma, Malaysia, Thailand and Singapore.

 Show your understanding

1. Describe Singapore's location in the world.
2. As Singapore is so close to the equator, what do you think the weather is like there?
3. Interestingly, Singapore has very few rivers and lakes. How do you think it gets its water?
4. Look at the picture of Singapore opposite.
   - Describe what you see in the picture.
   - What do you think Singapore would smell like?
   - Imagine you lived in the one of the buildings in the picture. Write an email to your Scottish cousin describing the difference between Singapore and Scotland.
5. In your own words explain why chewing gum was banned in Singapore.
6. Use the Internet to find out what might happen to you if you broke the law in Singapore.

53 Can you buy organic gum?

What are we exploring?

By the end of this section you should be able to:

▶ Explain how Chicza chewing gum is part of a co-operative

▶ Describe how natural chewing gum is made

Organic and biodegradable chewing gum is a fairly new concept. It has taken five years to develop and only appeared on our supermarket shelves in 2009. The gum is called Chicza and its primary ingredient, natural latex, comes from the chicozapote tree harvested from within the Mexican rainforest. Chicza chewing gum is managed and run as a co-operative.

Activate your brain cells!

Can you name a fairtrade product for every letter of the alphabet? For example **A** is for apples, **B** is for bananas, **C** is for...

What is a co-operative?

A co-operative is a group of people who get together and set up a democratically controlled enterprise based on common economic, social and cultural needs. Co-operatives tend to be not-for-profit, with any money that is made being shared with its members or re-invested back into the business.

Chicza gum is managed by the Chiclero Consortium, which is made up of over 56 smaller co-operatives in an area of 1.3 million hectares of rainforest. The consortium includes 2000 chicleros (the people that harvest the natural latex from the trees).

Co-operatives such as the Chiclero Consortium are important as they are managed by local people rather than large multinational companies. The focus is always on high product standards combined with a really fair deal (working conditions and pay) for the people who work for the co-operative.

How do you get the natural latex from the trees?

The latex is harvested from the chicozapote tree. The chicozapote tree will not grow properly or produce latex if planted outside of its natural environment – and it takes years to grow in the first place!

Biodegradable

Chicza is 100 per cent biodegradable. Once it is disposed of (not under your desk!) it becomes dust in weeks and can actually improve the texture of garden compost!

1. The latex is extracted from 100 feet tall trees by making z-shaped superficial cuts in the bark.
2. These cuts zigzag down to a bag placed at the base of the tree.

3. The dripping sap slowly fills the bag with about 3 to 5kg of sap per tree.

4. To prevent harming the tree, the chicozapote is then allowed to rest for six or seven years before it is harvested again.

5. Liquid latex is then boiled, dehydrated and brought to a sticky paste, which is stretched, kneaded and moulded into solid blocks.
6. Each block is carefully marked by its maker so that the Chiclero Consortium know exactly which tree it came from and can make sure that trees are being used in a sustainable way.

7. The solid blocks are then melted together with natural waxes to create the gum base (see page 105). While it is still hot, the gum base is mixed with organic sweeteners and natural flavours before being pressed and shaped into chewing gum strips.

Just for fun: What happens if you swallow chewing gum?

One 'old wives' tale' says that if you swallow gum it will remain in your stomach for up to seven years, as it is indigestible. But according to several medical opinions, there seems to be little truth behind the tale. In most cases, swallowed gum will pass through the system as fast as any other food.

However, people have been hospitalised for swallowing a lot of gum – so don't try it too often!

 ## Show your understanding

1. Which continent does Chicza gum come from?
2. What is a co-operative?
3. Apart from Chicza gum, can you think of any other co-operatives?
4. Using your own presentation ideas explain how Chicza gum is produced.
5. What do you understand by the term 'fair trade'?
6. How does the production of Chicza gum add value to fair trade?
7. How does chewing Chicza gum:
   - improve the lives of the chicleros and their families
   - improve the environment of your local area?
8. Think back to the advert that you made in Chapter 51. How would you change your advertising campaign to sell more Chicza gum?
9. What is an 'old wives' tale'? What other 'old wives' tales' have you heard? Draw one in your jotter as a three-square cartoon strip.

Explore further

Find out more about Chicza gum at www.chicza.com.

54 Is chewing gum an environmental issue?

What are we exploring?

By the end of this section you should be able to:

▶ Explain the hidden cost to the UK of chewing gum

▶ Describe some of the ways that chewing gum can be cleaned up

▶ Suggest at least one solution for dealing with the UK gum issue

 Activate your brain cells!

- Have you ever spat out a bit of gum on the street? Go on, admit it ... Collect the class results and discuss them together.
- Write down five appropriate ways to dispose of chewing gum.

Chewing gum is the only expanding segment of the worldwide confectionery market and gum sales in the UK have increased by 47 per cent since 1999. There are more than 28 million gum chewers in the UK, who munch their way through 935 million packs of gum and dispose of more than 3 billion pieces of gum per year.

Unfortunately, research shows that between 80 and 90 per cent of chewing gum is not disposed of in a bin. Instead it is dropped, spat out or stuck to something.

Yes, this is all chewing gum and bubble gum!

The hidden cost of chewing gum

Did you know that it costs about three pence to make a stick of chewing gum and about ten pence to remove it from the street if it's dropped? In fact, the UK government estimates that it spends £158 million a year trying to clean up chewing gum in public places. Some independent researchers think that the true cost could be as much as three times this amount because businesses, organisations and educational establishments face the same clean-up problem.

Inappropriately disposed of chewing gum also contributes to other problems such as toilets, drains and water filters being blocked; swimming pools having to be shut; and carpets, flooring, furniture and equipment having to be replaced because they cannot be cleaned. The overall cost to the UK taxpayer is almost incalculable.

Also remember that most chewing gum isn't biodegradable. It finds its way into landfill sites – and in 2010 the amount of waste gum is predicted to be 1 million tonnes worldwide.

The UK's worst chewing gum black spot is Oxford Street in Westminster, London. An estimated 300,000 chewing gum deposits can be found there at any time – disgusting!

How can chewing gum be cleaned up?

Cleaning up chewing gum is difficult, time-consuming and very costly. It may involve:

Scraping: This can be effective on very shiny surfaces but on most outside surfaces, because the material is rough (concrete, cobble blocks, paving slabs etc.), the gum gets stuck onto the surface and can't be removed with scraping.

Chemical removal: Chemicals don't remove the gum deposits but they do soften the gum, making it easier to scrape off. The problem is that some gum removal chemicals can be toxic, have unpleasant smells and can also discolour the floor.

Pressure washers: Cold pressure water machines will not remove gum at all. Hot/ steam pressure water machines loosen and remove the top surface of some gum deposits but still leave the oily stain behind. Pressure washers can be very noisy.

Freezing machines: They work by using dry ice and are very expensive and very noisy to operate. They can also damage the surfaces of some floors by leaving stains behind.

Other solutions include:

Banning it: As they did in Singapore (see Chapter 52).

Education: The best way to deal with the gum problem is not to drop it at all, but this involves changing behaviour. Lots of people agree that education will be the only thing that can help us do this. Educating people to chew biodegradable gum (see Chapter 53) might also be a solution – but some people just don't find it as tasty as non-biodegradable gum.

 Show your understanding

1. If chewing gum sales have gone up by 47 per cent since 1999 approximately how many:
   * gum chewers were there in 1999?
   * packs of gum did they munch their way through?
   * bits of gum were thrown away?
2. Why is it so difficult to calculate the actual cost of chewing gum to the UK taxpayer? Think about the 'hidden costs'.
3. Make your own copy of the table below and fill in the advantages and disadvantages of the different methods of gum removal.

Type of removal	Advantages	Disadvantages
Scraping		
Chemical removal		

55 Do you have a problem with chewing gum in your community?

What are we exploring?

By the end of this section you should have:

▶ Made up your own mind if chewing gum is a problem in your school and community

▶ Collected some data to prove or disprove your theory

▶ Presented your findings in an interesting way

Lots of people think that chewing gum is a problem in schools – that's why it's banned in many educational establishments (and the whole of Singapore!).

We already know that it costs a huge amount to clean up and it's not very pleasant for the school cleaners who have to pick it off the undersides of desks. You might have been in the unfortunate situation where you have trodden in someone else's gum or even sat on some and ruined your trousers!

Activate your brain cells!

- Think about your best 'chewing gum' story and share it with the rest of your class.
- Discuss with your partner the best way to get chewing gum off a pair of trousers.
- Do you think that chewing gum is a problem in your school and local community? Share what you think and why with the rest of your class.

Let's investigate – survey

Do you remember right back at the start of this book (I know it seems like a long time ago!) when you were looking at surveys? (Chapter 3). If you really want to find out if you have a problem with chewing gum in your school it might be worth doing a survey to establish public opinion. Public opinion is when you gather enough data from a representative group of people to get a real feel for what most people think about an issue (there will always be some people who disagree).

Project ideas

How many people will you have to interview in your school to get a real feel for what people think? How many questions will you need to ask and what sort of questions will be best – multiple choice or extended answer?

Let's investigate – interview

As well getting the opinions of lots of people by doing a survey, it might also be worth speaking to a few key individuals in your school community about the issue in a bit more detail.

Interviews are great for this as you can prepare your questions in advance and really get to the heart of the problem.

Project ideas

Can you think of some people in your school community who might be good to interview about the problems of chewing gum? How about your teacher, head teacher, school janitor or one of your school cleaners? Maybe even your school head boy or head girl? Do you think any of these people would be good to interview? Why?

Let's investigate – desks

Project ideas

Part of any investigation should be trying to find out things for yourself. Let's start with your classroom desks:

- Have a look under all the desks in your classroom and count the number of bits of gum that are stuck there.
- You should now be able to work out the average amount of gum per desk.
- Remember it costs about ten pence to clean up every bit of gum – how much is it going to cost to clean your classroom?
- How many classrooms have you got in your school and if all the classrooms were the same how many bits of gum would there be?

Let's investigate – playground

Project ideas

Your task is to find out approximately how many bits of gum have been dropped on your playground or other areas near your school. You could do this in a number of ways:

- Work in a group, divide up the playground and then get on your hands and knees and count every single bit of gum that you can find in your area.

- Work out the size of the space that you want to survey, count the gum in one or two sample areas and work out an approximate number of pieces of gum.
- Come up with your own clever method of sampling.

Tackling the problem

One simple but innovative solution – Gummy Bins!

Gummy Bins are proving to be an extremely successful gum litter solution. Their quirky, eye-catching design makes them an instantly recognisable receptacle for chewing gum collection. The inventers of Gummy Bins think that they are starting to change people's behaviour by reminding the public that chewing gum is litter and that it is not acceptable to throw it on the ground.

So far the Gummy Bins have been successful in one trial area of London. Gummy Bins on lamp-posts reduced the amount of chewing gum dropped by 72 per cent over a six-month period.

Would you put your gum in here?

Project ideas

Gummy Bins: Using a map of your school decide where would be the best places to put Gummy Bins. Would the locations change depending on whether you had more or fewer bins?

Poster campaign: Design a powerful poster to highlight the issue of chewing gum in your school.

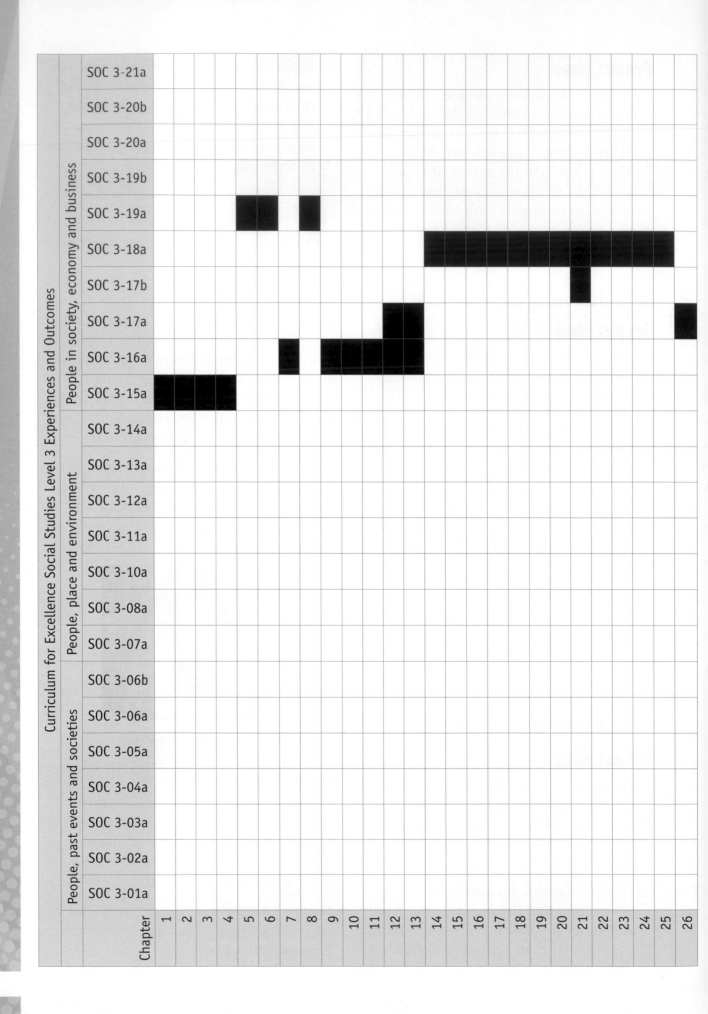

Curriculum for Excellence Social Studies Level 3 Experiences and Outcomes

	People, past events and societies							People, place and environment						People in society, economy and business										
Chapter	SOC 3-01a	SOC 3-02a	SOC 3-03a	SOC 3-04a	SOC 3-05a	SOC 3-06a	SOC 3-06b	SOC 3-07a	SOC 3-08a	SOC 3-10a	SOC 3-11a	SOC 3-12a	SOC 3-13a	SOC 3-14a	SOC 3-15a	SOC 3-16a	SOC 3-17a	SOC 3-17b	SOC 3-18a	SOC 3-19a	SOC 3-19b	SOC 3-20a	SOC 3-20b	SOC 3-21a
1															■									
2															■									
3															■									
4															■									
5																				■				
6																				■				
7																■								
8																				■				
9																■								
10																■								
11																■								
12																	■							
13																	■							
14																			■					
15																			■					
16																			■					
17																			■					
18																			■					
19																			■					
20																			■					
21																		■	■					
22																			■					
23																			■					
24																			■					
25																	■							
26																								

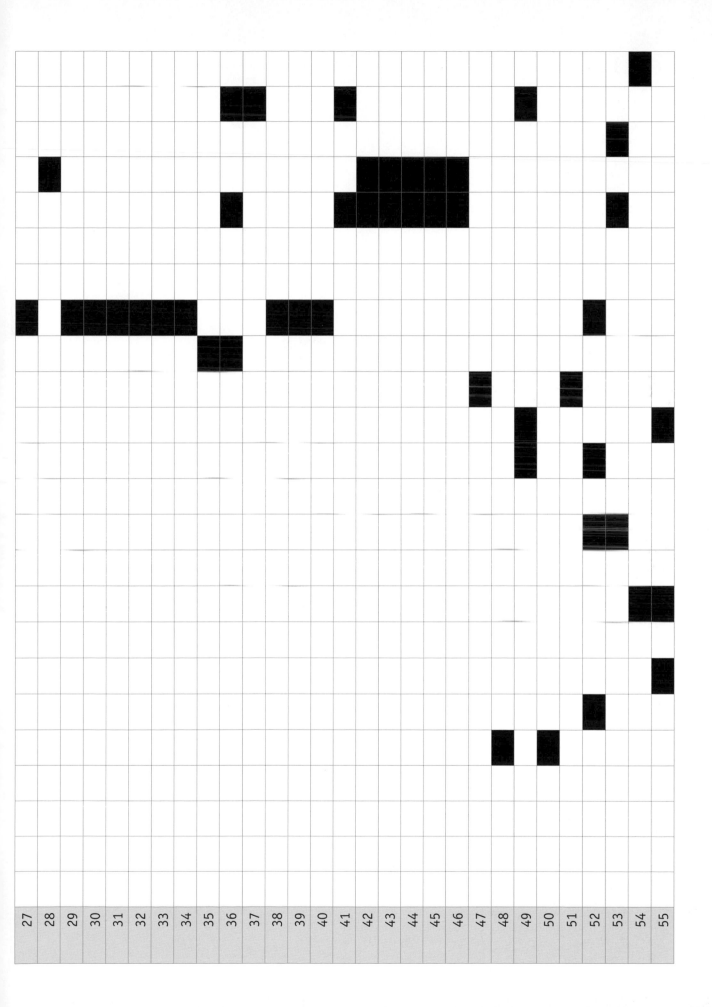